W9-BPK-590

Women and Their Emotions

REVISED AND EXPANDED

Women and Their Emotions

Miriam Neff

MOODY PRESS

CHICAGO

© 1983, 1995 by
MIRIAM NEFF

All rights reserved. No part of this book may be reproduced in any form without permission in writing from the publisher, except in the case of brief quotations embodied in critical articles or reviews.

All Scripture quotations, unless indicated, are taken from the Holy Bible: New International Version®. NIV®. Copyright © 1973, 1978, 1984 International Bible Society. Used by permission of Zondervan Publishing House. All rights reserved.

Scripture quotations marked NASB are taken from the New American Standard Bible, © 1960, 1962, 1963, 1968, 1971, 1972, 1973, 1975, and 1977 by The Lockman Foundation, and are used by permission.

The use of selected references from various versions of the Bible in this publication does not necessarily imply publisher endorsement of the versions in their entirety.

ISBN: 0-8024-9531-1

3 5 7 9 10 8 6 4 2

Printed in the United States of America

1983
Dedicated to the greatest expanders of my emotions . . .
our children
Valerie
John
Charles
Robby

1995
Dedicated to the greatest expanders of my emotions . . . still
our children
Valerie
John
Charles
and my youngest looking down on me requests to be known as
Rob

Contents

. . . .

Preface
A WOMAN'S
PERSPECTIVE

When I first wrote about women's emotions, I was motivated by the reality that most books written on emotions had been written by men. I read what men wrote about my feelings and found myself talking to myself: "But that's not how it is!"

In the decade since the original edition of this book, little has changed in Christian writing; men still do most of the writing about women. I recently browsed in a bookstore to discover new books on women's passions. Surprise—they were written by men.

And again, I found myself saying, "You just don't understand —even if you have listened to hundreds of women."

I see the world through a woman's eyes; I feel with a woman's feelings; I experience life in a female body.

Although I believe we've overemphasized physical reasons for differences in emotions, I believe we have vastly underestimated and ignored differences due to life experiences. When I wrote the original edition, I thought our different life experiences would move toward greater understanding.

I was wrong. The power struggle that originated with Adam and Eve rolls on. Women's life experiences are still incredibly different from men's. Our employment outside our homes has skyrocketed. Our rate of having babies has dropped. Yet the side effects of abortion, paycheck differentials, taxes, child-care, being household head (and hands and feet) have changed our world.

Does this affect our emotions? You bet!

I note in my original edition that I fumed over Kool-Aid spills. Now it's Perrier water, and who cares about spills?

Other crises challenge my emotions: a close brush with death for one of my children; being married—still—when statistics say that 90 percent of couples divorce when they live through the experiences my husband and I have shared.

Stepping back from the specifics of change I notice that what touched me then still touches me today. *Women still struggle with God's gift of emotions.*

Emotions are good and God-given. Not enough emphasis has been placed on the positive aspects of our feelings. We agree that the bumper sticker saying, "If it feels good, do it" is a fool's yardstick. But suppressing our feelings and living like robots with the emotional blahs doesn't honor God either.

A friend once told me that I am piggy on life and a glutton on living. So be it. My emotions are intense. As I write this, three white-tailed deer come out of the snowy woods outside my window. Their beauty is magnetic. Watching the rhythm of their flight is a near-tears experience. I want to feel, enjoy, and use to the fullest everything God has created in me—emotions included.

I want you to know that I do not write about emotions as an advice-giving counselor who has all the answers. Many writers have written from the counselor's side of the desk. It's comfortable there. I know the feeling—degrees nicely framed on the wall, referral numbers by the phone, a comfortable chair for the clients, and a box of tissues for the women.

But I have been the client as well. The other side of the desk is a different world. My tarnished spiritual halo is visible evidence that I am hardly the light on a hill I wish to be as a Christian. The pain of admitting my need for professional help, as an independent, self-sufficient person, is surpassed by the pain of emotional tangles. But I would rather be a tarnished Christian striving to live as the whole woman God sees than live as a victim of emotional tangles.

Battles are seldom fought alone: Victories are sweeter when shared. Do you think you are the only person whose emotions feel like the strangling tentacles of an octopus? "No temptation has overtaken you but such as in common to [woman]" (1 Corinthians 10:13 NASB). (The original word for man is *anthropos,* which means male or female, and as I said earlier, I see through a woman's eyes.)

You are not alone. Emotions can be transformed to become both helpful and useful. The victory of changing those strangling tentacles into strong, helpful arms is sweet. I'd like to share it.

Acknowledgments

· · · · · · · · · · · · · · · ·

I am surrounded by a great cloud of witnesses, women who have gone before as standard bearers. Dew-dryers: women who went first through the path of early morning wet grass and brush, shaking reeds in our path. They have plunged through soaked and shivering that I might come through dry.

Some I know personally and count myself privileged to call them my friends. Some I observe from a distance. They have been mentors to me though unaware of my admiration. Gifted teachers, preachers, writers, business women, students of Scripture, women with hearts for God—they have strengthened their feeble arms and weak knees and made the path more level for my feet.

Gail Meister, Linda Rios Brook, Margaret Nyman, Winnie Christensen, Naomi Cole, Dee Jepsen, Holly Coors, Janet McNicholas, Karen Burton Mains, Polly Hahn, Sherley Bott, Kay Arthur, Jill Briscoe, Mary Whelchel—I salute you.

Introduction

* * * * * * * * * * * * * * *

$\mathcal{E}$motions are a gift from God. Do you believe it? I confess that I sometimes wish I had no feelings. I'd rather be "blah," especially when the crowd is standing dry-eyed and indifferent as our national anthem is played at a game, and tears are streaming down my face. I picture our tattered flag still waving over an em-battled colonial fort, a blood-stained flag flying over a divided blue and gray nation, an ignored flag flying over our industrialized, mushrooming, wealthy country—a nation that God in His sovereignty has chosen to preserve.

I've wished I had no feelings as my irritation rises when machines answer my phone calls instead of people. I would prefer to be blah when a soccer fan of the opposing team shouts terrible things at my sons. I want to wield my umbrella in an unlady-like manner in close proximity to his vocal chords and inform him that my sons' defender moves are excellent in the eyes of their mother. I'd like to live without the nausea of my father's rejection and the aloneness and grief at seeing Mama's casket closed for the last time.

"Please color me *blah*, God. Emotions? A gift from You?"

Yes. If I accept the Bible as true—which I do—then creating emotions is God's doing. And He intended them for good. God is God; and God is good. I can come to no other conclusion than that He's a good Creator. How do we bridge the gap between His good intentions and our experiences? The answer would require an encyclopedia. But may I offer you this small book as a beginning?

I often hear that women are more in tune with their feelings and more sensitive than men. I'm not sure that this is true. I *do* believe we more frequently allow our emotions to lead us. Whereas men *think* about an event, we're sorting out how we *feel* about it. We live by feeling-based priorities.

The marriage of our minds and emotions equals what Scripture refers to as the heart. We bridge the gap between His good intentions and our experience by tenaciously connecting our minds and emotions and placing them both under God's control. Giving God one without the other is like half a bridge, which at best is little help and at worst is disaster.

Let's explore how anger can be positive, why Christians experience depression, and how good can come from these feelings. Let's discover how fear can be a valuable internal alarm system rather than a prison. Without boundaries, love on the loose has wounded women and destroyed their self-esteem. Yet the power of positive love is the greatest motivator that humans experience and the greatest healing agent God invented.

Are you ready to risk change? Are you ready to harness your mind and emotions together when they wish to race in different directions? Are you ready for a heart examination? May the words said of Nehemiah to our God be true of us as well. "You found [her] heart faithful to you" (Nehemiah 9:8a).

POPULAR, POWERFUL LIES

Before we begin, two lies need to be exposed. Perhaps you haven't fallen for them, but I have, and I am not alone.

One rainy fall day, I was speeding east to what I believed was Holland, Michigan. My daughter, her friends, and I were making great time. I would have bet my van and all the stuffed suitcases in it that I was on I-94.

"Toledo, Ohio—70 miles," Valerie stated, believing her information was good, relevant news.

"Can't be," I answered, "we're not on I-90."

One of my articulate passengers felt the need to enter the conversation.

"Val didn't say we're on I-90. She just read the sign that says we're nearing Toledo."

Silence.

Did it matter that I was 100 percent convinced that I was on I-94, destination Michigan? Hardly. The truth was, we were trucking to great music down the wrong road. Absolute truth existed. Facts didn't change because of my desire to believe differently. I had made a wrong choice.

Absolutes are unpopular today. Situation ethics, relativism, and our "if it feels good, do it" philosophy are all results of the widely accepted deception that there is no truth.

I write this book from the perspective that there is a Creator of all and therefore One who gives us absolute truth. Living by His truths will help you even if you begin with questions and doubts and are unsure that He can be trusted.

Women have been devastated emotionally by the lie that there is no truth. Like drought to our gardens and sub-zero winds to exposed flesh, the lie destroys our basis for good decisions and healthy living.

Where do we go when we have no working truth as our guideline? We have no facts on which to base our lives. We're on a trip without a map. We find ourselves in waves that at one point rocked us gently but are now getting rougher. Excitement turns to fear. We flounder reaching for something stable. Our lives are full of choices. Since we can't reach for facts, since there are no absolutes, we grasp for anything. What will guide our decisions? We act based on feelings. We don't have many options left. Feelings may be fickle, but they are all we have when we believe the lie that absolute truth does not exist.

Popular psychology has taught us that we are simple beings. Stimulus produces response. We are blank-slate blobs until we've created our own maze or have happened accidentally on an agenda worth living for. We are kind of special animals responding like robots to rewards, and sometimes we just can't help ourselves.

This lie is powerful. It transforms us from complex, God-created women who have wills that determine our destiny to kind of special animals. We act without realizing that our emotions *will* react.

We act believing our emotions can be disconnected. We believe Scarlett O'Hara's life verse: "I'll think about that tomorrow." We have been deceived to think we can postpone emotional consequences indefinitely.

EMOTIONAL SIDE EFFECTS

We do not act with our emotions in neutral. We are integrated, whole persons with emotions inextricably bound to our behavior— for better or for worse. Our emotions will respond to our actions— perhaps not now, or even tomorrow. We can predict some of our emotional reactions, but many will surprise us.

One of my sixteen-year-old students was pregnant. She did not intend to marry the father of the baby she carried. I advised adoption; however, she chose a solution to her crisis that would result in little disruption to her life.

Within five days, phone calls were made, the check written, and the appointment kept. Susan was no longer pregnant. Days of relief followed; her parents never knew. She missed a few days of school. She stopped seeing her boyfriend, but she knew she could handle that.

Susan believed that she had solved her problem. She had taken action, she had changed her circumstances, and everything was OK. She did not realize that her emotions would react. We now know that some women who experience abortion suffer emotional trauma.

Susan and I kept in touch. Her first time of trauma came when her baby would have been born. Seeing babies at that time depressed her. When there were no babies around she still struggled with guilt.

Susan married. When she gave birth for the first time, what could have been exhilarating, a time of marveling at the miracle of life, turned her world gray. She thought of another face that might have been.

I have precious friends who have had abortions. None of them made the decision lightly. Each was faced with what she saw at the time as an unlivable, unchangeable, bleak future. She did not believe she could bring a baby into her world to support, love, and successfully rear. And she did not believe she could give her child to another.

None of them realized the feelings that would surface later. Each has been surprised at the power of grief that grips her emotions at unpredictable times and in unexpected places. I weep with them that our world has become a place to which women increasingly fear bringing new life. Forty percent of American women believe the world is too bad to bring babies into. This belief affects our choices, the actions we take, and our emotions.

Women need to stand together and expose the lie that we can act with our emotions disconnected. We can no more will our emotions to "heel" forever than I could will the road I sped on to take me to Holland, Michigan.

We have allowed the world's idea of God to creep into our thinking. God is blamed for everything bad that humans can't control. For instance, on my insurance policy I see that tornadoes, earthquakes, damaging snowstorms, and trees falling on my house or car are "acts of God."

Yet I know that God's original intention for the humans He created in love did not include suffering. Look at Job's example. His children died; his financial empire toppled; his friends deserted him. Although his wife remained with him, she made his life miserable and urged him to curse God. To make matters worse, his body started to rot. "Through all this Job did not sin nor did he blame God" (Job 1:22). We can find truth in Scripture to guide each of our emotions. Living by these truths is vital to the healthy expression of each emotion. Believing God's goodness makes all the difference in the world.

Usually our attempts to manage our emotions are based on changing circumstances, rather than on actions based on facts. Rarely is such haphazard management successful for long—and no wonder. As one person, I have little power over some circumstances in my life. I can make choices and change myself, but I can't change other people.

Where do we begin when we hunger for changed feelings? We begin one truth at a time. We internalize God's facts and make choices based on them. Our feelings will follow. Emotions were never intended to be the lone basis for action. Action is to be determined by His absolute truth.

"If it feels good, do it?" Hardly. There is a better way. "The human mind plans the way but the Lord directs her steps" (Proverbs 16:9, author's paraphrase).

Chapter One
GOD LOVES YOU: TAKE IT PERSONALLY

Why do we feel, anyway? Why did God create us with emotions? Would we be happier if we had only intellect, not emotions? We wouldn't hurt, right?

TO FEEL?

What would happen if we were granted our occasional wish that we had no feelings? Besides not hurting, here's what would happen in my life. I couldn't cry with joy over red, wrinkled newborn babies. I wouldn't be stirred by emotion hearing Franz Liszt's "Second Polonaise." My husband and I would not laugh with delight over our baby's first wobbly step, or straighten in the bleachers as our son steps to the piano for his solo in the school variety show.

We wouldn't take deep breaths as the sun rises over the ocean. We would feel no tenderness or desire when our eyes locked with those of someone we love.

We would not be overwhelmed with awe when we round a bend in the Canadian Rockies and see the stark simplicity of rocks reaching for the heavens. We would not shiver with surprise when the "rock" beneath our snorkel masks is a sea turtle with textured feet that compel us to touch.

It's not that we don't ever want to feel. Of course, we want pleasure, excitement, joy, stimulation, love, and much more. Our quest for those feelings drives us to invest ourselves in relationships, hobbies, play, risk-taking, and sometimes work. If those positive feelings don't overtake us while we work, we work anyway —to pay the tab for what will produce those feelings.

We'd just like to change how we feel when we are uncomfortable or in pain.

OR NOT TO FEEL?

To be human is to hurt. We try to cope with hurt by walling off our emotions. "If I don't allow myself to feel, I won't hurt," we reason. True. But there's a better way. We need not grow a shell that keeps out hurt and all positive feelings as well.

Walling off emotions can lead to headaches, ulcers, substance abuse, sleeping or eating disorders, or a host of body-destroying addictions. You may not experience these, but one result is sure: You will be desensitized. You won't notice hurting people. Your pleasures in life will be limited as well as your hurts.

You won't see the sun clearly on a beautiful day. Looking out your window in the fall, you will simply see a square glass opening that probably needs cleaning. Instead, you could be viewing your very own panorama. You could be seeing greens mellowing into yellows, rusts, and crimsons. You could be seeing moss-covered branches punctuated by the stark black of old limbs.

You won't enjoy your children as much—nor will you enjoy anything as much, for that matter. Not feeling may reduce the hurt, but life is likely to be, to put it simply, boring. The biggest laughs and deepest joys will touch someone else's life, not yours. That is the price that desensitizing demands.

God had something good in mind when He made us with feelings. "I praise you because I am fearfully and wonderfully made;

your works are wonderful, I know that full well" (Psalm 139:14). David knew God had made a good thing when He created him. Do you feel you are emotional? David was. He was intense; he felt highs and lows. God said of David that he was a man after His own heart. Just maybe God has intense feelings too.

Tell God you know He made a good thing when He created you with emotions. Praise Him for your intense feelings.

WHY CHOOSE TO FEEL?

God loves you. We say it but don't believe it. "For God so loved the world. . . ." We don't take it personally. Sometimes I think falsely that God loves me because I love and have accepted His Son. I imagine myself in a throng of unworthy people crowded around Jesus, welcomed in God's presence because I'm with the right Person. That's true, but that's not the whole truth. There's something more, something better.

God likes me. He likes you. He delights in the personality blend He created in each of us. "For the Lord takes delight in his people" (Psalm 149:4). You're the only person like you He's got! I sometimes bear-hug my big teenage and young adult children and ruffle their hair. "You're the only John-boy I've got." And I call them by their special baby names (some of which, if I put in print, they'd be embarrassed forever!).

If they are leaving on a trip or going somewhere unsafe, I hug them extra hard and implore them to be careful. "You're the only Rob I've got." They get the message.

Imagine God hugging you and saying, "You're the only _____ (your name goes here) I've got."

You are different from every other person in the world. And God likes you that way. Do you believe it? Believing this truth is the first step and an absolutely necessary one to managing your emotions. If you can't accept your emotional makeup, you certainly can't manage it: You'll be too busy denying how you feel to know how you feel.

Are you a couch potato who loves to sit in your comfy chair reading? Do you enjoy a cozy fire and popcorn? Your Creator looks at you curled up in your robe, using your mind, toes snuggled in your fuzzy slippers, and says, "There's My daughter. I just delight to see her. She loves to read. I made her that way."

Delight: Proud Enjoyment

Have you ever watched a baby take those first steps? Mom applauds like her infant is an Olympic winner. Dad goes crazy with outstretched arms. Little feet wobble clumsily. Pudgy arms wave for balance. And PLOP! Down on the padded diapers two feet down the road of life. If you think parents make fools of themselves over such a minor accomplishment, do you know who's worse? Grandma! And Grandpa's a close second.

That's delight. God delights in us—just because we are His children.

I delight in seeing my son Rob water-ski. To me, he's so smooth. No professional skier could be more agile, have more balance than my son. Sometimes I just have to stand up in the back of the boat laughing and applauding! (No, I don't care what other boaters think.)

That's delight.

You bring God delight. It's not about accomplishments; it's because you are you.

If I can't accept how I'm wired up emotionally, I can't manage my feelings and enjoy living.

Judy was an emotional woman. She cried when she found a bird with a broken wing. When her husband was late for dinner, she poured the spaghetti down the garbage disposal. She cheered wildly when her son ran out on the football field, but she also ranted and raved over his jacket left on the hallway floor.

The phone rang one day. The call was from her daughter's high school counselor. Her daughter was in trouble. In the scene that followed that night, her daughter blurted out, "I can never talk to you. You can't listen, and you make a mountain out of a molehill. Let's face it, Mom. You can't cope."

Sobbing to her neighbor the next day, Judy said, "I just can't help it. I've always been this way. If I just weren't so emotional."

Judy had not accepted that her particular personality—emotions included—was good and God-created, and she had not learned to control her emotions instead of letting them control her and using them to control others. When her emotional intensity made her miserable, she tried to suppress her feelings. With her high energy level, she could have managed her household efficiently and pursued a career or volunteered. But she burned out lots of energy on tantrums and manipulating people to do things her way. She did not manage her emotions; they managed her. As Judy began to thank God that He liked her, she found herself manipulating others less. Manipulating hoists a sign that says, "Please make me look like I am somebody special." When a woman realizes that she is special, she doesn't need to carry a sign saying so.

Power: From God's Heart to Yours

Once Judy accepted that her emotions were intense, she began to recognize her strengths and weaknesses. Like a powerful river that needs boundaries so it won't flood, she needed to learn control. She discovered that she was especially sensitive to negative input and needed to limit "bad news" in her life. She reduced the amount of time she spent reading newspapers, shuffling through the crises and gore of the day. She read a weekly news magazine that saved time and didn't focus on disasters she found unprofitable to dwell on. She reduced television input: Cut-down comedy and violence were on her "bad news" list.

Judy made another important discovery. She had creative potential that had been bottled up and frustrated. Feeling insecure, she had not explored ways to express her creativity. When a person is busy trying to look important, she can't afford failure. And expressing creativity usually demands the risk of failure.

As Judy took her attention off herself, she found she could sense others' feelings easily. She could detect another's tiredness, discouragement in a friend, hurt in a relative. She was a good encourager. Energy that had been burned out before on impulsive anger and hurt feelings could be rechanneled. The effect was like recharging a battery that had once powered a tiny flashlight and now was strong enough to run a lighthouse. Judy found more satisfaction in knowing she'd helped a friend than in soothing people she'd hurt by having a temper tantrum.

Emotional women and men usually have potential for creativity. David was a feeling person. As an accomplished harpist, his music soothed Saul. He wrote poetry expressing his moods and life experiences. Though centuries have passed since he wrote the psalms and our cultures are vastly different, we still feel with him as we read. His words parallel our lives. Common emotions span our canyon of differences. "Save me, O God, for the waters have come up to my neck" (Psalm 69:1). My version when I'm feeling depressed: "Help me, Lord, I'm goin' under!" The eighth psalm describes how I feel about God.

David's life had extreme highs and lows. (Read 1 Samuel 16 through 2 Samuel and 1 Kings 2.) At one time he led an exuberant dance in the street. After his son's death, he grieved. "And the king was deeply moved and went up to the chamber over the gate and wept. And thus he said as he walked, 'O my son Absalom, my son, my son Absalom! Would I had died instead of you, O Absalom, my son, my son!'" (2 Samuel 18:33 NASB).

Under David's leadership Israel began its climb to power and greatness that would be climaxed under his son Solomon. Though David was a great military man, credit for his victories belongs with God. But God used David! Creativity became military strategy. Israel's economic progress didn't happen from chaotic good luck. Planning the temple and gathering the materials resulted from David's intense love for God within the boundaries of organized action.

Compassion brought crippled Mephibosheth to the king's table, even though the young man was the grandson of Saul, David's enemy. Tradition would dictate that Mephibosheth, an heir of David's rival for the throne, be killed. Instead, David brought him into his family.

David's love turned to lust when he ignored his emotional boundaries. Like a powerful river bursting over its banks bringing devastation, David's lust for Bathsheba was lethal. We see that lust brought adultery, murder, the death of David's infant son, and intense grief.

We cannot help but see that the same intensity in David's feeling usually resulted in good. We can wish on David an unfeeling personality that would have avoided sin, but that would have also denied the blossoming Israel a creative, dynamic king. Saul would not have experienced compassion at the hand of the one he hated and threatened with death. Israel's neighbors would not have witnessed the power of Jehovah-Jireh's right arm. Solomon would not have had the opportunity to learn at the knee of a creative father. David, full of vigor, creativity, strong desires, and above all, love for God, was the person God wanted him to be.

Genesis 1:27 tells us that we are made in God's image. We are patterned after Him. Our creative Maker delights in each feeling person He has made.

Nobody's Clone

Does acknowledging that our emotions are God-given solve all our problems? Of course not. In fact, we have a new problem. We are different. We are unique. And still in this decade, being positively one-of-a-kind is given lip service only. Humans continually wish to be like other humans—to blend in. Radical is weird, not special. But you and I are not called to be somebody else's clones. We're called to be women in God's image.

Are you glad that you feel? Aren't you glad you can cry? Don't be ashamed of those tears. God collects them in a bottle (Psalm 56:8). (For some of us He must have a huge jug!) Aren't you glad you can laugh? Do you ever listen to people laugh? Some chuckle, some roar, some giggle, and some shake all over in silence. Forever infectious, laughter is another mark of God's creativity in us, His audible way of saying, "See? I made you different!" I'm sure He chuckles when He hears us laugh.

Accepting that our emotions are good and God-given is the beginning of feeling good about our feelings. Let's look at each emotion separately. What's good about anger? Why did God create us with the ability to feel guilt? What good can come from depression? How can these emotions be positive energizers in our lives? We'll look at eleven emotions from a positive perspective.

Then we'll look at how to break bad emotional habits that have grabbed us. Tangled emotions do not automatically untangle. If you want to grow a step further, read the chapter on discipline. God loves us. I hope what I write helps you take it personally and feel the feeling.

Chapter Two

ANGER: THE LOOSE MISSILE OF THE DECADE

uring the Persian Gulf War, we sat in our living rooms watching smart bombs enter with precision the specific rooftops of designated buildings. Before our eyes, the targets exploded: Energy connected with its object; power accomplished its mission.

Imagine the same energy gone berserk—exploding anywhere, everywhere with no direction, no mission. Bombs on the loose. I believe anger has become the emotion on the loose in this decade.

When I first wrote *Women and Their Emotions*, I believed depression was women's most destructive emotion. Anger has taken the lead. While depression immobilized us, anger in women today is poisoning us. Lethal anger in others is destroying our world, our families. Anger commits murder, destroys property, plots revenge, and changes a sweet mouth to a poison-dipped dagger. It is the seed from which bitterness grows.

Recently a zealous Jew gunned down fifty-three Arabs in a mosque in Hebron. Bitterness had grown for a lifetime in his soul.

My sister remembers our father telling her not to come home again because she was involved with a young man of another race. Anger had planted its seed.

Unresolved anger can produce long-term depression. Battered children, battered wives, burned-out cities, and destroyed nations are its by-products.

I thought in 1983 that arsenals and technology combined with anger in political leaders would destroy our world. My opinion has changed. Power-hunger within, not anger, fueled by threats between nations is destroying nations. They are dying from within. Arsenals are sitting in cobwebs while countries crumble from within. And often hunger for power drives the internal death machine.

EXPRESS OR SUPPRESS?

Shouldn't an emotion this destructive be suppressed? Isn't this an emotion that should be walled off and denied room in our lives? The pain that anger brings might be reduced, but the good that can result from positive anger would also be eliminated.

Jesus experienced anger and the result was good. God feels and expresses anger. We cannot say it is a bad emotion or that Christians shouldn't feel it. The ability to experience anger is part of our being human image-bearers of our Creator.

Anger is an energizer, a stimulator. Anger increases our physical power. We can choose the option of channeling anger in a positive direction.

An old myth prevalent in some Christian circles is that anger is sin. The evil one has chuckled over that myth and used it against women. If I believe that lie, when I feel anger I shove it under— sweep it under the rug, Grandma would say. Maybe you put it in a backup file as I do. Anger sneaks out from either place.

Suppressed anger throws no hairbrushes, cuts off no people in traffic and spouts no nastyisms to our customers, our bosses, or our children. But our stomachs knot, our blood pressure rises, and we perspire buckets when adrenaline floods our system.

Anger's Boundaries

I read, "Be angry, and yet (#1) do not sin; (#2) do not let the sun go down on your anger" (Ephesians 4:26 NASB). *How, Lord?* I ask. I'm heading down the wrong highway with my anger. How do I get to the right path?

God gives us two clear boundaries to channel anger:

1. Don't do the wrong thing when you are angry.
2. Acknowledge anger and act appropriately within twenty-four hours.

Let's look at the first boundary. When can we be angry, and for what reasons? Look at Jesus. He was being harassed by the Pharisees. They made him angry. No, He was not sinning. He couldn't sin. He was experiencing a God-given emotion. He had every right to be angry at their criticism. They were a step behind Him trying to undo everything He did.

Jesus was not angry at their opposition or the inconvenience of their disruption. He was on a mission to do His Father's will. And He was doing it. He wasn't angry because He feared they would stop Him.

He was angry at their stubborn hearts (Mark 3:5).

He was disappointed (to put it mildly) by their attitudes.

The Pharisees' misplaced values triggered His emotion. These leaders protected laws, not people. They cared about appearance, not reality. Protecting their prestigious positions at any cost was their mission. His anger was well-directed—right on.

Misdirected anger—anger for the wrong reasons—often begins with misplaced values. I was often tempted to value neatness and unscratched furniture above my developing children. This misplaced value is deceptive because it's true that our children should grow up with pleasant, clean surroundings. But when we allow things to take precedence over people, we've gone too far. Twisted values produce anger for the wrong reasons. When our children run with muddy feet over our newly-scrubbed floors, we can tell them that they are dumb and inconsiderate—that we slave all day for their benefit, and they return the favor by acting like a bunch of animals—or we can teach them to be careful and thoughtful of others' work.

Misplaced values make us angry at revolving doors that don't revolve, long trains that keep us waiting at railroad crossings, and "holding patterns" at airports. I believe the supreme objective of the world is to get me where I'm going on time.

I first wrote this one afternoon when fate had ignored my schedule. That very morning I ran out of gas in 94° Chicago heat with a friend and two preschoolers in tow. In ten minutes my daughter would be coming from orchestra practice to a locked house. Empty gas tanks are never a convenience. I never schedule "inconvenience" time in my calendar.

And now I write somewhat irritated that my portable phone has fritzed out and someone backed into my car last night. It's true progress that this intense writer finds these inconveniences only mildly irritating. I've made progress, but I still have a long way to go.

You may, as I do, feel anger that women are underrepresented in higher positions in your workplace. Anger is misplaced if I value position for the sake of power. It is appropriate if I desire benefit to people by women using their God-given gifts.

Too often I am angry for the wrong reasons. You may, as I do, feel anger when someone bumps your "I am important" sign. Women are not alone in feeling that anger. It's a problem to both sexes. We have been taught to react differently than men when we feel the adrenaline from being bumped, but the sign reads the same. When our self-esteem is based on something we have, we get upset when someone takes that something away. Our feelings of self-worth are based on who loves us or likes us. The person doesn't love us anymore—or even like us—and we become angry.

What makes us angry? Anger can begin when we feel people haven't treated us as we deserved. Our twisted value says "I'm important because I'm somebody, and I want all of you to treat me that way." The fact is that I'm important because God made me and I'm His. Period. Reasons for anger change immensely when we realize that foundational truth.

Anger's Power

Feeling the adrenaline of anger and misusing it can become a bad habit. Ruffled feathers feel good. A few outbursts bring a sense of power. Subordinates scramble, clerks speed up transactions, our mates hurry to please, coworkers clear a path. We discover a new tool to get our way. We use it. Anger is a powerful tool.

Humans need not be taught to use anger to their advantage. Give anger a little room and it blossoms profusely. Proud of our temper? Some are. "I get mad; then I get even! You'd better watch out!" We let people know so they will be ready to let us have our way as soon as our face gets red and a snarl twists our lips. Before long, we lose the ability to set boundaries to use the adrenaline of our anger for positive purposes. We don't use anger; it uses us.

Like a Mack truck rolling over people, squashing their feelings, damaging children's self-images (permanently, except for the grace of God), sometimes abusing our children, we excuse ourselves because we lost our temper. The results of allowing the habit of anger to grow are ugly and destructive. Who can reason with a person who has refined this habit? Who can match words with her? Verbal battles become one-sided barrages. The angry person's decibel level is hard to match. Her senses are dulled, and she has no concept of the feelings she trucks over. A few nastyisms become a verbal arsenal of dehumanizing, crippling bombs that are released at the slightest, most feeble reason.

Anger's Ripple Effect

Some say she's hurting herself more than anyone else. Not really. Consider the expanding circles of anger. Five years, ten years. Discouraged clerks, berated police officers (who may have a hard time enjoying their jobs anyway). Add the mate who withdraws more, medicates more, maybe deserts.

Then there are the children.

They feel inadequate, they are told they are nobodies. Angry parents berate their children just because they are there—and small. Mom can't stand the sight of them; she can't wait until they leave home. Their developing minds reach a settled conclusion: "I'm really rotten. What a zero I am."

This misdirected anger is behind much child abuse. The circle widens. The child who grows up with that picture of herself will at some time in her life stand and say, "I am somebody." It may be with gun in hand, though men more often use guns. It may be holding a bottle or using drugs. It may be by using her body to see if sexual experiences make her feel special. It may be by continuing the cycle with her own children. The angry person doesn't bear the greatest unhappiness from anger. Suffering accumulates in every life she or he touches.

In 1993, sixty-one children were killed in Chicago. If this fact does not belong in a chapter on women's emotions about anger, where does it fit? In the newspaper interviews where reporters vie for shock value and emotion, it is usually the mother photographed in tears in disbelief that a gang or senseless, meaningless violence has taken her child. She questions what more she could have done to protect her child.

I ask, Why not seek out the father? Why are these women carrying so much grief and anger alone? Children are always created by two. Where's Dad? AWOL since conception? Did he abandon his family's real world for the numb world of alcohol or drugs? Did he leave a hollow space for another man to fill, maybe a man who would be jealous and intolerant of the children? Why are these women weeping alone?

POSITIVE ANGER: THE TRUTH ABOUT ANGER

For those of us who are intense, regardless of the cause of our anger, we must ask, Where do we go from here? When, at whom, and how can we be positively angry?

Truth: We Can Be Angry at What Angers God

Jesus was angry at stubborn hard attitudes.

He was angry at pretenders and manipulators.

He was angry when people misused His Father's house.

He was angry at selfish behavior and greed.
God was angry when people ignored His rules.
He was angry at injustice.

What did Jesus do when He felt angry? I would like a simple answer, a pat formula to that question. I haven't found it in the Bible yet.

Sometimes He took aggressive action. In His Father's temple He created a ruckus, flipped furniture, and used the "big stick" technique for communicating His message. Sometimes He asked quiet questions in response to obnoxious harassment. Other times He bluntly called people fakes. When His own disciples were arguing about who was the greatest, which no doubt galled Jesus, He taught them a kindly, informative lesson.

In other words, Jesus taught us by example to choose what action is appropriate when we are angry.

Women designed with unique personalities, individualized emotional control panels, with no two bodies alike, express their anger in different ways. We make different choices in different circumstances. That's OK.

Beverly LaHaye was angered at the changing political climate in our country. God's value of children, families, and life were not only being ignored: Our government was undermining their safety with laws and policies. She started Concerned Women of America which is now a half million strong, and that voice in our capitol is heard by hundreds of politicians.

Her action based on concern for children has been much different from mine. My husband and I adopted two children. My anger at our nation's deplorable neglect of our most treasured gifts motivated me to meet with Congressman John Porter and confront him regarding his safeguarding baby seals with greater zeal than he was safeguarding our children.

Sisters, let's give each other room to take different courses of action. Let's not judge each other for being different.

I have never picketed an abortion clinic. But I have hugged teen girls in my office after they have had abortions, when they weep and can tell few people of their pain.

I resigned from our educator's union because the national arm lobbies for issues that violate my religious convictions regarding the role of public schools in birth control. The union also advocates homosexual teachers. Yet I have Christian sisters who hold leadership positions in the union and intend to be catalysts for change. We are called to express our convictions in different ways.

Truth: We Choose What Action
We Take When We Are Angry

Has your anger ever caught you off-guard? An event, the sight of a person, a sound triggers feelings more intense than you can understand? Answering these questions might clarify what's happening inside.

1. Have I reacted with insecurity to mistreatment?

Concentrate on how special you are to your Creator.

Anger reduction may include looking in the mirror every morning and saying out loud, "I am important because God made me and loves me. No person or circumstance can change my importance or reduce my value by anything they say or do." If I do not connect that mental truth to my emotions in my moment of anger, I'll do the wrong thing. Why be angry at people who put us down? When we realize how special we are to God, little threatens us. As maturing, godly women, we can see the person who puts us down through eyes of compassion. We can pray, "God, reach into her life and reassure her of Your overwhelming love. Remove her need to strike out and hurt."

2. Can I make a plan to act on what triggered my anger?

Pick up your calendar and schedule step one of your plan.

Your plan of action may not change the event or person. It is your willingness to act and your motivation that matter to God. Jesus didn't convert the Pharisees into honest people. His Father's house was misused again. His disciples behaved pathetically *after* His teaching. (And John Porter didn't vote the way I advised him to!)

We are responsible for obedient action when we are angry. We are responsible for placing boundaries around our emotion of anger; God is responsible for the outcome.

3. Will my plan result in good, or am I out to get even, to polish my tarnished "I am important" sign?

My ultimate goal for this action is _____, and I have verified with Scripture that God will be honored if this goal is achieved. When I'm unsure of my own motivation, and I'm brave enough to admit it to God, He's bold enough to show me what's real. He shows me what's God-pride, and what's Neff-pride. He shows me what's love-driven and what's self-driven.

4. Whose approval am I seeking?

Paul says, "But to me it is a very small thing that I should be examined by you, or by any human court; in fact, I do not even examine myself. I am conscious of nothing against myself, yet I am not by this acquitted; but the one who examines me is the Lord" (1 Corinthians 4:3–4 NASB).

5. Is my feeling extreme or intense, given the circumstance?

Have your emotions been pumped by childhood experiences, crises, or special hurts? Mine have. You may be able to discover the connection and control your intensity level. It's a tremendous struggle for me. I usually cannot keep my anger in boundaries until I know the connection and understand why the event or person has pushed my hot button.

When I first wrote on anger, I couldn't write about some of my hot buttons and failures. Dirty laundry? pride? Maybe both. I also felt protective of my mother and father as if talking about the pain of my childhood would betray them.

I recently read in Scripture that we suffer so that others may benefit. I was struck by the recognition that keeping secret my childhood pain kept me from helping women who need to know that God is bigger than our secret scars. I tell the following failure on my part that you may benefit.

I always fought with my husband while taking him to the airport for business trips.

Connection: I had the same feeling of abandonment that I felt as a child when my mother left and my father gave me little attention.

Fact: My husband was not abandoning me. For those who know my husband, he would abandon his wife, or his work, or his kids, when a belching volcano and an arctic glacier register the same temperature. My anger was due to a wrong connection.

I have learned from many of my friends that we expect our husbands to act like our fathers did. Wrong connection. For those of us who had poor relationships with our fathers, anger will rock our marriages.

Getting professional help may be a necessary key in discovering connections in our lives. The discoveries, though sometimes painful, are precious. Recognition enables us to channel our anger in positive directions, forgive old hurts, and enjoy the present.

6. Is my anger feeding on worry, becoming a greedy monster of my energy?

Peace comes from trusting that God is in control (Isaiah 26:3).

Work and exercise keep anger in its boundaries. (P.S. The workaholic, driven-to-distraction person will be an easy target for negative anger.) We each find our own pace. Exercise is a proven tool for anger control. Adrenaline that cannot be used at the moment in a positive direction can be left on the running path, the exercise machine, or the aerobics mat.

7. If I think my anger has gone hyper, what will help me gain control and cool off?

Take a walk. Get into nature. God's therapy through His creation has more than double-digit return from watching waves crashing, aspen leaves dancing, robins pulling on elastic worms. Feel the wind. Dig in the dirt. Follow a butterfly.

Search for reasons to be thankful.

Truth: Take Action or
Make an Action Plan by Nightfall

God's direction for our emotions is *always* healthy for our bodies. No wonder, He created both. He knows that anger and sleep are not comfortable in the same bed. God intends sleep to restore our bodies. Using adrenaline depletes us.

When we're angry and plan to act positively, often we cannot take action within twenty-four hours. Simply having a plan will give you peace when you can't act immediately.

STEPS TO TAKE

1. Make a list of what angers you.

2. If God would be angry at the item, put "Act" beside it. Justifiable anger will energize your action list.

3. If anger is self-motivated or power-driven, put "Self-Search" beside it.

4. For each "Act" item, make a plan of action to change what angers you, or at least affirmatively live your Christian conviction.

5. For each "Self-Search" item:

   - Ask, "How can I be thankful for this person/circumstance?"
   - Plan an appropriate response in advance of being at places, in circumstances, or with people who anger you. Your goal is to regain control of your misdirected anger.
   - Write a Bible verse on an index card for each "Self-Search" item. When your anger is triggered, take time to read the verse.
   - Find a hobby, activity, or exercise to divert anger while you're in the process of learning to redirect and control your emotion.

6. Thank God for the positive potential of anger: motivation for our mission for the next decade.

· · · · · · · · · · · · · · ·

The Lord is good to all; he has compassion on all he has made.
All you have made will praise you, O Lord; your saints will
  extol you.
They will tell of the glory of your kingdom and speak of your
  might, so that all [women] may know of your mighty acts and
  the glorious splendor of your kingdom.
Your kingdom is an everlasting kingdom, and your dominion
  endures through all generations. The Lord is faithful to all his
  promises and loving toward all he has made.
The Lord upholds all those who fall and lifts up all who are
  bowed down.

*The eyes of all look to you, and you give them their food at the
proper time.*

You open your hand and satisfy the desires of every living thing.

Psalm 145:9–16

Chapter Three

BITTERNESS: ANGER'S LEFTOVERS GONE SOUR

*B*itterness is anger's leftovers: moldy, dried up and crumbly, a powerful emotion gone sour. Bitterness is the toxic waste of anger. How does this toxic waste get in the heart of a Christian woman today?

I have a friend who is a productive, giving, Christian woman. She models a sweet, gentle spirit and is a godly mentor to Christian women who begin their own businesses as well as to women in media. Yet she battles bitterness every day. Divorced after forty-seven years of marriage, surprised, and devastated, she could not comprehend that her marriage was over.

Bitterness is not an emotion God created in His original idea, His first two perfect human beings. Scripture speaks of God and Jesus being angry. Yet I find no evidence of Them experiencing bitterness. Not a God-given emotion, bitterness is a feeling that sprouted like a weed after human beings said "No, thank You" to their Creator's guidelines for living.

As I write, I ask, Who cares? Does it make any difference whether it's a God-given emotion or just a nasty feeling we have? Anger and bitterness can *feel* the same. Who cares about the origin of these look-alikes?

We must know the difference for our spiritual survival.

My experience the last ten years has taught me that identifying and separating anger from bitterness makes all the difference in my world. Anger is like a river that can feed its territory when kept in boundaries. Its power can carve granite, bring beauty to the most desolate space. Kept under control, anger is like a pruned, life-giving fruit tree or a wheat field that multiplies productivity.

Bitterness is like sticker weeds that choke out good plants, boiling water on yeast that kills growth, toxic cholera-producing bacteria in our drinking water.

Anger can be channeled to empower us. Bitterness must be rooted out, destroyed. It never does us no good, no way! Its most common shape is hatred. We cannot manage hatred until we have managed bitterness. When we kill bitterness, hatred usually dies of natural causes or goes up in the same smoke.

"How do I keep it from growing?" we ask. Apply a simple biological truth: Dead roots don't grow. Destroy the roots of bitterness.

I also picture bitterness like a flattened ghoulie that likes to hide under the tablecloth when relatives get together. Brother can sit across the table from brother with bitterness rolled out between them. "He got the breaks I should have had. He got the attention that my parents should have given me." (Of course, women don't think like that!)

"If they financed me like they financed her . . . "

"If I'd been the youngest . . . "

Like sharing a bad cold at the table, spouses get infected, and eventually children and cousins get hooked in.

Bitterness fits snugly over the board table at church. Since few women sit there, we can resent the men. "He has more clout, and I work harder."

Women who *do* sit there can become bitter. "So few voices join me to speak for our needs! You just don't understand!" One sister eyes another, an employee her fellow-worker (especially the boss's favorite). You may think bitterness bothers only the down-and-out. But rich, favored women feel it as well as women who have been busted by life.

Scripture tells us not to let the bitter root grow and defile many (Hebrews 12:15). The One who made me knows bitterness will make its way into my system and be a trouble-maker.

How did the bitter root get there?

TOXICITY DUE TO NATURAL CAUSES

Picture a hospital nursery. Tiny little bundles sleep in rows of aquarium-like cribs. They are different already (though behavioral scientists don't like to admit it)—some are boys, some are girls, some are ruddy with piercing dark eyes and a halo of straight dark hair. Others have pastel pink scalps glowing without a trace of hair. Some sleep twenty-four hours and open one eye when hungry. Others catnap between fussing and fuming. Feeding time, in their opinion, should be a continuous twenty-four hour process.

Differences aside, each little person is identical in one way. Invisibly tattooed across every baby-soft chest is a sign that says, "I Am Important." Each child will attempt to prove it is true by her life experiences, especially if she does not realize that God created her and loves her. Any person who interferes with the process will fertilize the bitter root. Some gather wealth; others build a reputation by knowing the right people, appearing at the right places, or by doing "In" things. Some choose to be sex symbols or to be extreme in dress and personal appearance. Call it "clout," "influence," "prestige," they gotta have it.

What happens when someone cracks a rung on our ladder to success? We become bitter. Parents become bitter toward their children because the children's behavior brings humiliation.

I well understand the temptation. Believing myself to be a successful mother of four preschoolers, I proudly deposited child #1 at the kindergarten door. No problem.

Later (I can't reveal how much later. Sergeant Friday said on Dragnet, "The names have been changed to protect the innocent." I add, "The date is classified information to protect identifying the guilty."), I climbed off my matronly Schwinn bicycle, complete with basket and child seat, lifted off my son, and deposited him near the line of eager scholars. They followed Mrs. Bean, as Park Ridge children had been doing for twenty years, to kindergarten wonderland complete with the "green bean machine," Big Bird, and the alphabet family. He didn't follow eagerly.

I coaxed, bribed. Mrs. Bean soothed and wooed. My son revealed deficits in preparation-for-school parenting.

The kindly principal appeared, assured me he was good in these situations, and picked up his new student. My son bit his neck.

I heard through the grapevine that this was a first in Mrs. Bean's memory and the last time the kindly principal tried to carry in hesitant students. (It was not my last lesson in parent humiliation.)

Today, as a high school counselor, when teens are in trouble and I ask parents to meet with me, I understand when the parents don't want to come to school. Some are bitter at our system; some are angry and bitter at their kids. Their I AM IMPORTANT signs have been tarnished by their children's behavior.

Women become bitter over failed business. We may be bitter that life has not worked out the way it should have when we carefully constructed our goals and followed the steps to meet those goals. We can become bitter over unreturned love: our lover's, our child's, or our parents'.

A church in our area surveyed its attenders and discovered that one in six adults had had a sexual relationship outside marriage within the previous three-year period. General surveys of women indicate they often give sex in order to feel likable and accepted. "Somebody finds me appealing." Teen girls tell me they thought they'd feel "more grown up." They expect to feel popular and special.

Not so. The short-lived ego boost, if it exists at all, becomes the long-term hurt. "He didn't love me enough to marry me." A lack of commitment hammers in the message, "I've been used." I wish I could write so eloquently and with such vivid influence that

I could convince girls, teens, and all women of this vital fact about our emotions: *Sex without respect, mutual commitment, and the covenant of marriage will at some time crush your self-esteem and flatten the boundaries of your anger.* Bitterness is unavoidable though we may hide it under an "I didn't care anyway" attitude.

Look again in that hospital nursery. Each infant wears another invisible sign. It says, "I AM DIFFERENT." Wander through an art gallery, shop at a craft fair, watch a girls' soccer game. Different is good. Diversity and healthy competition result. But diversity and competition can also breed bitterness.

PREVENTION, THE BEST SOLUTION

Our Creator gives us three truths to prevent bitterness.
1. We are created by the Best, for the best.
2. God is our covenant lover, even when love flows one way only—from Him to us.
3. We are adopted daughters because Jesus loved us enough to exchange His life for ours so we could call His Father "Papa."

TOO LATE FOR PREVENTION: TREATMENT NEEDED

Do you believe the facts of prevention with great conviction at one stage of your life, and then find yourself questioning or forgetting them? I do. Life is unfair. You and I know that. I still have a hard time accepting that fact. I get angry and hold my anger in silence until bitterness sets in.

My mentor, Winnie Christensen, recently reminded me that when life is not fair, I need to remember God has not promised that others will love me as I feel I need to be loved. My efforts may go unrecognized and unrewarded. And yet, *no bitterness allowed.* Being bitter is being angry at God.

In my heart as I listened, I protested, "but I've never loved God more!" I pondered her words and eventually their truth dawned. All bitterness is rejecting God being God in my life.

God has simply promised to meet my needs. He hasn't told me how, through whom, or when. To expect people to do what only God can do guarantees bitterness ahead.

When life is unfair, I can choose two guaranteed-to-cure, one moment at a time, treatments: good grief and forgiveness.

If it is hard for you to grieve your losses, you are surrounded by women with the same malady. I'm one. We may cry easily, but grieving is more than shedding tears. Our culture does not grieve well. We're supposed to keep a stiff upper lip. (Whatever that means!) Strong women get on with living. Only the weak pause.

Grieving means identifying what we lost. I don't mean what other people think we lost. I mean, when our door is closed, when it's us and the mirror, what are we missing and why? I did not grieve my mother's absence from my family during my teen years. I replaced Mama—cooked, cleaned, mothered my younger sister—and got on with my life.

Then a light went on. I was always looking for a mother. I needed a wise older woman who would show me how to mother my precious, vivacious, ever-changing child.

The time had come for me to grieve my loss before I could go on. Good grief meant saying, "God, I know Your Plan A didn't include Mama being gone. It hurt. I know You care about my hurt. The one I expected to show me how didn't, maybe couldn't."

Why is bitterness so often mixed with relatives?

My "Titus woman," Polly Hahn, taught me a valuable lesson. "We expect more from our relatives than we do from our closest friends," she explained. I could see that in my own life. Even when a relative hardly knew me, I expected his or her support and sympathy. Common blood transfuses no extra sensory perception. A marriage certificate does not deliver understanding.

You and I may assume closeness in our relationships that comes only with time and shared experiences. Many women during their grieving space have taken comfort from these words:

"For my father and my mother have forsaken me, but the Lord will take me up." (Psalm 27:10 NASB)

"For your husband is your Maker, whose name is the Lord of hosts." (Isaiah 54:5 NASB)

"'For the mountains may be removed and the hills may shake, but My lovingkindness will not be removed from you, and My covenant of peace will not be shaken,' says the Lord who has compassion on you." (Isaiah 54:10 NASB)

Lost (Disappointed, Redirected?) Expectations

I'm still sorting out the connection between expectations, anger, and bitterness in my own experience. The process takes a lifetime.

I come to peace and acceptance that life isn't fair in one season of my life, or in one of my roles. But somehow my large wisdom in one season becomes infinitesimal in another. I came to peace with the unfairness of life in my childhood. I even made a list of the strengths that developed through unfortunate stuff. But the pesky weed took root again. I found myself bitter that my son is bipolar.

My child.

Why my child?

Shouldn't children come into this world with the right chemicals in their brains so they can live? work? attach to other people? marry? support themselves? have healthy babies?

Why? Why? Why? Not just my son, but all the children.

I don't know why. But when I weep for what my child cannot do, for what he is not becoming, when I grieve that his loss is my loss, somehow my bitterness disappears, at least for the moment.

Let me tell you a secret. My "weeding practice" when I grieved my childhood losses was good practice. With each year that passes, I relinquish more expectations. Today I told a friend I am at peace regarding my son. Progress.

Forgiveness

Forgive. This simple seven-letter word holds the key to every successful relationship: friendships, marriages, business partnerships.

Forgiveness is a two-way street. But it works if one lane is blocked and the action is on one side only. My father died in 1987, oblivious to the devastation in my life due to our relationship. I forgave him the summer of 1980. I forgave him again kneeling beside his coffin. I can still be crushed by a memory.

Don't wait for the person who let you down to come and ask for forgiveness. It may never happen. Forgiveness means I agree to bear the pain, surrender the loss to Jesus' care, accommodate the knife in my back or in my heart. I will be free of hatred; I will be free of bitterness. In our humanness we may think it impossible. It is hard, but not impossible.

Some of us have an "unforgivable" space reserved in our hearts. For one person, it may be money lost through a relative. In another case it may be bankruptcy with other people involved. The space always has *people* in it.

When I gave up my space marked "unforgivable" (the hole in my heart left by my father), God filled it with three surprises. First, I saw my father as a person to be pitied rather than as a man of power. Through a conversation with his brother I gained insight into the life he led that created the person he became. I saw his misery through eyes of mercy. He was, indeed, a person impoverished, to be pitied rather than feared.

The next surprise was to discover that I felt love for him. I began to give him room to be human and imperfect.

The final surprise was that his power to hurt or control my life was gone.

When forgiveness cures bitterness, ugly features soften. The Old Testament describes it as beauty replacing ashes, bathing in glad oil instead of tears, dressing to celebrate instead of to mope. I compare it to the transformation of volcanoes underwater to the beautiful Hawaiian Islands.

CLASSICAL BITTERNESS

The story of the prodigal son's return illustrates classical bitterness.

"Look," said the elder son, in keeping with his birth order behavior. "I've worked, I've followed you in the family business, I do what you say. So, where's *my* party?

"He's invested your hard-earned money in worthless junk bonds. And you are celebrating?"

Translation: "Dad, you should be polishing my I Am Important sign."

And his father answered, "Everything I have is yours."

Translation: "You missed the point, son. I have enough for you. There's plenty."

Translation to women today: There is no limit to the supply as far as your Father is concerned.

When Jesus told this story, He wanted to illustrate the Pharisees' bitterness. Jesus' spiritual power and charisma were obvious. Common people were learning from Him. Sick people got well. And the Pharisees were sulking.

"We're the leaders here," they said as they pushed and shoved trying to get to the head of the crowd following Jesus and ahead of Jesus even, so Jesus would follow them.

Remember Jonah? He sat outside Nineveh predicting destruction because the people were bad. They changed. Jonah sulked.

What if the people stayed bad and God sent fire bolts like He did on Sodom and Gomorrah? The result would be: big guy Jonah, what a man!

But God forgave. People praised God, not Jonah. Poor Jonah. He sulked, he pouted, he complained. Reading Jonah 4:5–9, I keep seeing the phrase "God provided." God provided a vine (it wilted), a worm, and a scorching east wind. I am sure Jonah did not believe God was providing for his needs.

But He was. Jonah needed at that season of his life to learn that God's priorities were unique. God's emotions were unbalanced: His compassion was stronger than His anger. His hunger to save His people was insatiable. And He specializes in second chances. I'm glad to know that. I hope you are too.

STEPS TO TAKE

1. Look at what makes you feel important.

2. Why should you feel important?

3. If you are bitter, toward whom and why?

4. Grieve your loss. (See the chapter on grief including the steps to take, pages 145–46.)

5. Are you willing to surrender the loss and forgive?

6. Ask God to love the person. (In His amazing way, sometimes He loves the person through us while we're healing from hurt. At the same time, we are healed by exercising forgiving love.)

7. Ask God to show you your "unforgivable" spaces.

. . . .

Relent, O Lord! How long will it be? Have compassion on your servants.

Satisfy us in the morning with your unfailing love, that we may sing for joy and be glad all our days.

Make us glad for as many days as you have afflicted us, for as many years as we have seen trouble.

May your deeds be shown to your servants, your splendor to their children.

May the favor of the Lord our God rest upon us; establish the work of our hands for us—yes, establish the work of our hands.

Psalm 90:13–17

Chapter Four

FEAR:
THE POWER
OF COURAGE
OR COWARDICE

*M*y sister was sleeping in her city apartment. She woke to something cold and hard lightly touching her cheek. A dark form hovered over her; another moved in the shadows behind him searching her apartment. Disgusted at finding nothing valuable, the one in the background said, "Take her."

"If you make noise, I'll kill you."

She felt the cold knife move to her neck. A rough hand ripped her panties. As one man violated the boundaries of her territory and possessions, the other prepared to violate the boundaries of her own flesh. A scream rose inside her that she could not suppress even if it meant death would follow. Her attackers fled.

Having no phone, she ran to a neighbor's house to call the police. When they arrived, her apartment had been bolted closed from the inside. The attackers had returned expecting to finish what they started. Her apartment had been ravaged, but not her body.

A new kind of fear moved into my sister's heart and mind. No longer a vague nagging sense of discomfort, her fear now had real shadows, the cold touch of steel. She could have been immobilized by that feeling. The choice was hers.

Women's fears come from dramatically different sources, but the emotion feels the same for all of us. I hope as you read and learn of other women's fears, events you've never experienced, crises you will never face, that you empathize with your sisters.

We need *sister* unity. I believe women have a great weapon against negative fear: empathy for each other. When we feel the fear together, we unify. Some women's survival depends on it.

I am greatly encouraged to pick up my newspaper and read of unified women who have opened shelters and started businesses to employ other needy women including the homeless. Women are networking and reaching out to each other. We are moving beyond fear.

DECADE OF CHANGE: CAUSE TO BE A COWARD

What's different about the fear women have felt in the last decade? Violent crime jumped 5 percent in 1991. Nearly 25,000 Americans were murdered. Prisons are overcrowded, so judges ease the pressure by releasing even violent offenders. Severe violence is a chronic feature of 13 percent of marriages. It takes an average of thirty-five battering incidences before a wife will file a police report against her husband.

Fifty percent of children who grow up in battering families are physically abused. This is more than a statistic to me. Last week in my job as a counselor in a public high school, I spent one day meeting with different small groups of teen girls. More than half of them had been abused, and some now get into fights with their mom or dad in order to protect a younger sibling. One teenager sat with his back straight, one fist clenched in the other hand, and told me, "He don't beat me no more. I'm bigger than him and I broke his ribs last time."

Women feel fear. Christian women feel fear. Some fear for
their grandchildren, their parents, their children, or themselves.
The causes have changed due to circumstances, age, and stages in
our lives. Being employed/not being employed may put us in unsafe
places including more deserted residential neighborhoods. Violence, rape, pregnancy, street conditions where our children play,
public transportation—the list of changes during this decade is
endless.

I used to fear moving. Strange dark doorways, sounds that
creak in the night, the whoosh of a furnace going on, water drip-
ping: All might be fearsome forces coming to get me in the night.

Some women suffer panic attacks. Mental health professionals
define this as a common reaction to extreme stress. Although we
don't fully understand what causes people to suffer this extreme
fear, we do know that twice as many women as men experience
panic attacks. Common sense tells me this is logical given the difference in safety between a woman's world and a man's world. For-
tunately, 60 to 70 percent are helped by medication. Although I
am pleased there is medical treatment for the symptoms of fear, I
hope we can change the causes that produce fear.

Have your fears changed? Mine have. This emotion challenges
us to learn new strategies. But we still begin to manage this emotion by recognizing it is God-given and can be positive. This basic
emotion is necessary for survival. Newborns fear loud noises and
loss of support. If we are driving or walking near railroad tracks
when the train whistles, fear results in action. Fear keeps us from
leaning too far over bridges, climbing in the animal cages at zoos,
and speeding down a foggy highway.

Eric was a student who seldom experienced fear. This void in
his emotional makeup got him into lots of trouble. One time he
broke both wrists experimenting on his motorcycle. One of his sci-
entific "inventions" blew up his neighbor's lamp post. After he told
me of a trick he played with fire, I told him he would never make it
to age twenty-five. He laughed. I was serious.

I met his mother in an antique shop a few years after he had
graduated. At that time he was in the hospital recovering from

another experiment. He had built a glider. In order to increase its speed he tied it to a friend's car. They were speeding through a forest preserve; the car rounded a bend, bringing a grove of trees between the two vehicles. Eric crashed. A little fear might have prevented that.

Fear is a valuable emotion. Changes in our ordinary world can shape us into cowards or stimulate courage. Courage can be learned by choice. And fear can be a source of strength and motivation.

FEAR THAT FREES US OR FEAR THAT SMOTHERS

The word *fear* in Scripture has three different meanings. Each offers us a valuable truth as well as a solution to managing fear.

1. *Phobos:* healthy fear, reverential respect for God, fear that motivates us to act in a positive way.

"Since we have these promises, dear friends, let us purify ourselves from everything that contaminates body and spirit, perfecting holiness out of reverence [fear—*phobos*] for God." (2 Corinthians 7:1)

The same word, *phobos,* is used in Acts to describe the reaction of Christians to miracles demonstrating God's power.

2. *Eulaheia:* caution leading to reverence.

"Therefore, since we are receiving a kingdom that cannot be shaken, let us be thankful, and so worship God acceptably with reverence [fear—*eulaheia*] and awe." (Hebrews 12:28)

3. *Deilia:* cowardice. This emotion is not God-given.

"Peace I leave with you; my peace I give you. I do not give to you as the world gives. Do not let your hearts be troubled and do not be afraid." (John 14:27)

How do we know the difference in our lives? Which fear do we feel? These questions help me sort out my fears:

1. Does the fear immobilize me?
2. Does it keep me from serving others or obeying God's calling or direction in my life?
3. Does my fear focus me inward on my own sense of strength or competence?

If I answer "Yes," my fear is *deilia*—cowardice. And God has a solution for me. The woman who appears to be in the greatest control of her environment may be the greatest coward. She may fear being in a space where she does not control the circumstances or people around her.

4. Is my fear accompanied by a sense of being smothered and restricted?
5. Is my fear triggered by a person or circumstance?
6. Does my fear keep me from going to new places, trying new experiences, meeting new people?

These fears can be valid and appropriate at one time in a woman's life, but they are usually destructive if they become permanent. Like anger, there's a time restriction. Scripture tells us the "times-up" button sounds within twenty-four hours for anger. I have not found a specific time-buzzer for fear in Scripture, but I suspect that God intends us to take our fears to Him first.

Fear can motivate us to positive action, but it will become negative if we do not act. It can become a web that tightens over time. I was refreshed to meet a seventy-year-old woman traveling in Israel. She takes a few trips a year to expand her mind and broaden her interests. I did not ask her about her fears when she travels, but I'm sure she's felt a few. I'm equally sure that they don't control her.

While we know that God never intends an emotion to smother us, let's give women—our friends, relatives, and coworkers—room to go to God and become free on their own time schedules. I am tempted to judge other women's speed of becoming free. I forget that when I first wrote on fear, the sound of the furnace in the night froze me to my sheets while I perspired buckets.

7. Does my fear tingle with the excitement of the unknown?
8. Does my fear demand action, though I do not know the outcome?
9. Does my fear coexist—comfortably—with peace?

It's from God! Feel the fear and act anyway!

Treating the Symptoms/Treating the Cause

I fear that some therapy today for frightened women is treating the symptoms, not the cause. When you believe you cannot change the cause, you must live with the symptoms. True, if we cannot change the cause, treating symptoms is better than nothing. I know we sometimes benefit from medication. Support groups have meant survival for many women including two of my three sisters.

My wish for all women is that medication and support groups be temporary: temporary because places are safe and/or women are strong. My advice to frightened women is, "Get all the help you can, dear sisters!"

But dream with me a moment.

What if we had power to prevent what causes fear in women today? "For God has not given us a spirit of timidity, but of power and love and discipline" (2 Timothy 1:7 NASB). What might we accomplish?

Empowerment is a good word for Christian women. It means feeling confident to act with authority. Having authority is part of being an image-bearer of God Himself. It means that your judgment is sufficiently respected by others and yourself to act based on your decision.

Visualize women with unified power changing our often empty churches into safe places for battered women to go. (Even if the batterer worships there.)

Visualize our women modeling the Sarah Bradys, Dee Jepsens, and Kay Coles Jameses, who have devoted years of their lives to fighting gun violence, pornography, and discrimination.

Empathy for our frightened sisters' plight has been the power behind many positive programs. Empathy empowers us.

Apathy, on the other hand, strips us of motivation. We cover our eyes and ears to our sisters' fears. In a recent self-defense class, women were told to yell "Fire!" when they needed help. They were told that when women yell "Help!" people keep their distance because they fear getting involved. Yelling "Fire!" gets people out and at least curious. Sadly, empathy in humans is becoming a scarce emotion.

Let us not lose heart.

I hope the day will come when Christian women empowered by healthy reverential fear of our loving Father will lead the battle against the fear that is smothering and destroying our sisters.

STEPS TO TAKE

1. Recognize that the spirit of fear (*deilia*) is not from God. Victory begins by recognizing the opponent. Read the story of Esther to get a good look at courage. She faced fear with the stress of the survival of her nation on her shoulders. Instead of shuddering and staying uninvolved, she said, "If I perish, I perish" (Esther 4:16).

2. Ask God for the spirit of power (2 Timothy 1:7). I remind myself that *just because I don't feel it doesn't mean I don't have it.* He gives what He says He'll give. When I do not believe I have His power, I depend on my own—which is pathetic at best. When I feel powerless because of big government, longer waiting lines, depersonalized living, and the hyperactive evil one, I'm defeated.

3. Connect love and fear (*phobos*) in your mind; they are inseparable. Hard to do, isn't it? They seem a mismatch. Disconnect love and fear (*deilia*); they *are* a mismatch. "There is no fear [*deilia*] in love, but perfect love [*phobos*—healthy reverence for God] casts out fear" (1 John 4:18). "But now, this is what the Lord says—he who created you, Miriam, he who formed you, Miriam: Fear not. . . . Do not be afraid, for I am with you" (Isaiah 43:1, 5, personalized version). Put your name in this verse.

    When I'm afraid, in my mind, I climb onto the lap of my Father/Papa. He holds me with strength and compassion. I hear Him say, "You are loved by Me. Rest secure here. I will shield you all day long."

4. Build discipline into your life. I must talk to my age-mates for a moment: Discipline is not a thing to resist. You know what I mean, don't you? During our impressionable adolescent/young adult years, we just were not into it.

    Since discipline means teaching, if we're teachable, we can still become disciplined. Discipline is not a straitjacket. It's learning. It's choosing the habit of reading the Bible, praying, and fasting.

If you are younger than forty, I don't know what the word "discipline" means to you. But I do know it's a gift from God because He says so. And we need it in order to live reverently bold lives without being cowards. We are to be continual learners, alert women (1 Thessalonians 5:8 and 1 Peter 5:8). "Be alert." That means use the minds He gave us. He expects us to be wise. Ultimately, our faith crowds out fear.

· · · · · · · · · · · · · ·

I lift up my eyes to the hills—where does my help come from?
My help comes from the Lord, the Maker of heaven and earth.
He will not let your foot slip—he who watches over you will not
*   slumber; indeed, he who watches over Israel will neither*
*   slumber nor sleep.*
The Lord watches over you—the Lord is your shade at your
*   right hand; the sun will not harm you by day, nor the moon*
*   by night.*
The Lord will keep you from all harm—he will watch over your
*   life; the Lord will watch over your coming and going both*
*   now and forevermore.*
                    Psalm 121:1–8 (A song of ascents)

Chapter Five
. . . .

CONTENTMENT:
THE ELUSIVE
EMOTION OF
THE DECADE

*L*et's take a video camera to a street corner in your city and interview women passing by. Chicago, Toledo, Detroit, Beverly Hills, Dogwood, Nashville, Little Rock, Missoula—here we come.

"Excuse me. Do you have two minutes to answer a few questions?

"How do you feel today, Ma'am? We're doing a survey on women's feelings of contentment."

Of course, while we are asking, our camera is recording answers as well as facial expressions. What answers might we hear?

I imagine the following:

"Am I on TV?" Smoothing her hair, our subject leans charmingly into our camera lens.

"Are you doing this for 'Sixty Minutes?' Sounds like an Andy Rooney thing. What's the give-away?"

"Please. Do you really think I have time for this?"
"Are you contented?" we ask. "If not, why not?"

MARKED BY CONTENTMENT

My dictionary tells me that contented women are radiant, joy-ful, glad, exuberant, happy, secure, jovial, and pleased. Let's take our survey tapes back to the VCR and tabulate our findings. Con-tented. Not contented. Reason. What will our survey show? Are women contented? Why or why not? What did the women in our survey say? What did their body and facial language say?

Any valid survey would require that we move from our street corner to a few other locations. As I write this, if you and I were on a corner in Chicago, we'd be happy to move on. It is 10° below zero and the wind chill factor is −41°.

Responses might be better if we spoke to women on vacation: on beaches, at Disney World, on fishing boats in Northern Wis-consin. Even that could be risky, though. Recently a mother of three children assaulted and threatened a flight attendant on the family's return flight from Disney World. Apparently vacations do not guarantee contentment. I remember when my husband and I took five children all under eight years of age to the World's Fair. Remaining memories are delightful, but in the snapshots, Bob and I are lacking that contented look.

Maybe we should give up the roving interview idea and stand at the magazine rack in our local grocery store. What do the glossy covers tell us about contented women? Obviously, a contented woman is attractive, unwrinkled, and in control of her life, her man, and her hair. If you buy the magazine you may also find contentment.

I am convinced that whether we compile our data by conducting interviews, measuring what women buy, or examining any other indicator that explores contentment, we'd discover that external *stuff* monopolizes women's quick ways to seek contentment. Money, health, and appearance top the charts.

Another barometer of contentment in women might be what women do with their time. Work, hobbies, and volunteering would surface as sources of contentment or lack of it.

CONTENTMENT
· · · · ·

Is a woman's feeling of contentment different from a man's? I don't think so. I believe our God-given emotion is the same. Female babies and male babies are born with the capability of feeling contentment. What differs is the message our culture sends us: "In," "Politically correct," "Role/Right," "Our Place." Those messages, combined with our individual life experiences, families of origin, gifts, talents, and physical differences, all greatly affect how we feel. The quality of contentment differs in women and men by the time they reach adulthood, not necessarily due to God-given differences in our emotions at birth, but due to life experiences.

Women and men alike lack contentment with their appearance. Wishing to be a different weight tops the list for both genders: 75 percent of women and 57 percent of men wish they weighed less.

Both sexes can feel discontentment because of their lack of power and influence, career success, or the accomplishments and appearance of their children. In fact, we can lack contentment for any reason. How, when, and why we experience the feeling is as varied as our personalities and the spaces we live in.

POTENTIAL FOR CONTENTMENT

If we could separate Christian women from others, would we find a difference? I wish I could tell you that Christian women are more contented than women who are disconnected from their Creator. We have that *potential*, but contentment is not always our experience.

For example, Christian women who are employed outside their homes are disaffirmed by their churches. The network of believers who should support and encourage us often do not. Women who are not Christians and who do not attend church often have a host of networks that encourage them to develop their potential through their work.

Content with Our Calling

Studs Terkel stated, "I think most of us are looking for a calling, not a job." In a survey I am conducting, Christian women indicate that their work is their calling. Every morning when I enter the hallway at the public high school where I work, I believe I am being obedient to my Creator's calling for me, not just showing up for my job. Although the Christian employed woman may not experience contentment from the support of others, she is contented with God.

Research is surfacing that gives us a glimpse into why Christian women do what they do and how they feel about it. A recent study by a Christian organization found that homemakers and working women (women employed outside their homes) are beginning to realize they cannot be or do everything. However, that is the only issue from the survey on which these two groups agree. Let's look at what they said.

> Homemakers do not think a woman can combine a career with family responsibilities, consequently only half believe women should have a choice to work outside the home. In contrast, the vast majority of working women think that women should have a choice to work outside the home. Also they know by experience, especially full-time working moms, that they can combine careers with family responsibilities.

> Nearly all homemakers say they have chosen to stay home because they want to be home with their family. Another major reason is because they think it's too difficult to juggle a job and a family.[1]

Since a woman's contentment is affected by whether or not she feels supported by others, these two groups differ. Women who are not employed outside their homes feel supported by others. Fewer than four in ten full-time working women with children feel affirmed by their pastor or church members for their decision to work.

This fact should send an incredibly important message to churches: Ignoring the needs and feelings of working women risks further misunderstanding and alienation. Women entering the workplace is one of the greatest trends of recent years. And the change will probably continue. According to the U.S. Department of Labor Women's Bureau, by the year 2000, 85 percent of women between nineteen and fifty-four will be employed. Women will make up the majority of the work force.

If you were a working woman feeling affirmed at work by knowing it is your calling and by positive interactions with your coworkers, feeling disaffirmed at church by the messages sent judging your priorities and intent, how would you respond? If you have a few discretionary minutes, where would you spend them? If you have a little extra energy, where would you invest it? I fear that if churches continue to send their message of disapproval to the working woman, churches will lose significant, vital members of the body.

The elusive feeling of contentment may evade women who are disconnected from their Creator. That's expected. If a woman doesn't know the One who created her, she can't follow the tailor-made operating manual for her life. As Christian women who know our Creator, contentment can *still* escape us.

Women in Scripture, including Rebekah, Sarah, and Martha, struggled to believe they possessed all they needed to feel content. They struggled unsuccessfully with what they wished for and did not have. Jealous and envious, they became manipulative and sometimes bitter. We know that Martha found a better way. She changed from the harried complainer to a believer who still served but with a new spirit (John 11:24–27; 12:2). She connected with her Creator.

Contentment Is a Choice, Not a Discovery

My Bible dictionary tells me that contentment means:

1. a perfect condition of life in which no aid or support is needed
2. sufficiency of the necessities of life
3. a mind content with its lot.[2]

Number one is out of the question for us, humanly speaking. And number two is 50/50—maybe, assuming you are healthy, can work, no person in your family has a debilitating disease, and catastrophes of nature and economics don't shake your world. Contentment looks out of reach for many of us until number three.

Contentment is a state of mind. Feeling contented is brain-controlled, not emotion or hormone controlled.

"But godliness with contentment is great gain. For we brought nothing into the world, and we can take nothing out of it. But if we have food and clothing, we will be content with that" (1 Timothy 6:6–8).

"Keep your lives free from the love of money and be content with what you have, because God has said, 'Never will I leave you; never will I forsake you'" (Hebrews 13:5).

It is clear from Scripture that Christian women are not to seek contentment in possessions and objects. God's teaching is radical. He tells us that we have Him and that's enough. That's radical contentment.

We can know if we meet the mark by looking at what discontented women feel. They are conceited, and they provoke and envy others (Galatians 5:26). If I am conceited or envious, I am not content.

We can know we've missed the mark if we don't like our place in life. We are free to change our place in life if we can, but if we cannot, we are to be content where we are (1 Corinthians 7:17).

When I think about my poor farm girl heritage, I envy other women. I remember the farm sale in our front pasture after we lost the farm. The big old Minneapolis-Moline tractor with a few patches of bright yellow left sold for $100. I sagged against a tree in disbelief. It seemed like a friend on whom I'd perched for hours in the hay fields—worth so much more. Poverty. When I moved to the city, I hoped to keep my poor roots secret.

I became a Christian and began to read the manual of the One who created me. I read of Paul, who had the right roots but landed in prison. If Paul could be cold, hungry, in prison—and content, my farm girl heritage should make me feel like a queen. I always had food and shelter. And I had freedom to wander through hills and bluffs with white-tail deer, shaded by persimmon, walnut, and tulip trees. I can choose to see my roots as poverty or riches.

Contentment is a matter of the mind. It's perspective. It's making a list of what we believe will make us content in one column, writing as many pages as we wish, then, in the opposite column, writing simply, "God." The "God" column more than balances our other list, no matter how long the first column is.

I WILL BE CONTENT IF	ANSWER
1. _____	God
2. _____	God
3. _____	God

WHY CHOOSE
TO BE CONTENT?

Are you surprised at James's statement that "where you have envy and selfish ambition, there you find disorder and every evil practice" (James 3:16)? "Every evil practice" is serious stuff. When we read our Bibles we see graphic examples.

Amnon, King David's son, was not content with his love life. He wanted his half-sister. His friend Jonadab helped him plot his rape of Tamar. Result: Amnon's brother Absalom had him killed. King David responded. Eventually 20,000 men were killed, and that did not end the cycle of evil.

Sarah could not bear the discontentment of her childlessness. Abraham did not resist her urgings. The result: Abraham's seed produced a family tree ultimately divided into the Jewish and Arabic nations. My newspaper today documents a tiny portion of the results. They have been at war during every decade since. Recently a Jewish medical doctor, using an automatic rifle in a Muslim mosque, killed forty-five people and then was beaten to death by the crowd.

The root of envy makes a widow look yearningly at a couple eating dinner in a restaurant and think, "Why not her? Why me?" The same root of envy keeps a father from listening with enthusiasm while his friend tells of the touchdown his son scored. Envy keeps parents checking on the scholastic success of their neighbors' children and keeps an employee from wanting his coworker to do a really good job.

Envy is not the protective feeling we may have for things that are rightfully ours; it is "the feeling of displeasure produced by witnessing or hearing of the advantage or prosperity of others."[3] This "feeling of displeasure" never dies of natural causes. It is always cancerous. Sometimes it expands a small injury into an ugly, abnormal growth, with external results. When we react with displeasure after hearing about someone else's advantage or prosperity, we are feeling that *we* should have that advantage, that break, or that bonus. How do we know that what is advantageous for another would be good for us?

A child sits in his sand castle by the lake, building and patting, pouring water, and imagining. An envious child looks on in gloom. A jealous child destroys the sand castle. Rebuilding it will bring smiles back to our little construction engineer, but it will not remove the knot in the other child's emotions.

There is no room for envy in our lives when we believe Romans 8:28, that all things work together for good. An effective beginning is to tell the truth to ourselves.

STEPS TO TAKE

1. Admit the truth (James 3:14). "Lord, I envy _____." We may have to add, "Lord, my envy has turned to jealousy, and I don't want him/her to have _____. I've been secretly wishing _____ would happen to him/her."

2. Accept your differences (Romans 12:3–6). "Lord, help me to use and enjoy the abilities, gifts, physical strengths, and material things You've given me. What I lack is not a problem to You, so I won't let it bother me."

   This exercise may help you: List several things about you for each category:

   My apartment/home is: (example: convenient, cozy)
   My physical strengths are:
   My abilities include:
   My gifts include:

   Lynda Rider, a pastor's wife and mother of three, while living next door to the church completed the list this way. My home is: easy to maintain, convenient to my husband's work, church, library, and stores; very low cost to live in.

   My physical strengths are: mind (can learn and think), cooperative hair, clear skin, healthy, strong (can work hard all day), decent weight (can maintain it "fairly" easily).

   My abilities include: talking with people, making friends, encouraging younger women, speaking, sharing, organizing and decorating a home, and gardening.

My spiritual gifts include: exhortation.

(Childlessness, disappointing to her at one time, motivated them to adopt three children and her gift of exhortation has been strengthened and expanded.)

Carol Adams, legally blind and a mother of two, had this response:

My home is: [Contrast: damaged by water in excess of $56,000—under repair for six months] roomy, I can move about freely without bumping into things, an older-generation home, I can express my old-fashioned tastes in decorating, I can walk to church, the train, downtown, and my close Christian friends' homes from here.

My physical strengths are: [Contrast: 5 out of 180 degrees sight; hearing impaired: loss of 80 percent in one ear and 50 percent in the other] strong will and constitution. I do not give up easily, working hard to maintain normal life functions.

My abilities include: standing my ground when I believe something, avid reading, homemaking, and letter-writing, sharpened sense of perceiving other people's feelings.

My spiritual gifts include: encouraging women in small ways like notes, a listening ear, praying for others. I have served in the church nursery, Sunday school superintendent, I can dig into the Bible to prepare for sharing.

Both women thanked me for asking them to do this exercise. They were encouraged by focusing on the positives in their lives. Lynda was packing their family of five for a three-week vacation and Carole was sitting in her water-damaged home.

3. State your trust that God's working in your life will result in good (Romans 8:28). I can still say, "Lord, I can't see how _____ will ever be good. But I trust You."

I need to search until I find something good—even if it is quite remote and not on my high-priority list. This may not be necessary for you. Contentment is more elusive for some of us than others. Step 3 is a hard one for me, especially when I face losses I did not expect.

I can tell you that losses I *still cannot understand* have forced me to fill the void with new interests, hobbies, and people. And in my weakness people, including myself, are blessed.

4. Praise God—because He told us to. Do you have scars on your body? They can remind you either of past hurts or the miracle of healing. I think that's why, when Jesus came to life again, He kept the scars on His hands. Visualize His hands. Remember Jesus' words to His doubting follower: "Put your finger here; see my hands. Reach out your hand and put it into my side. Stop doubting and believe" (John 20:27). Give yourself permission to be scarred and feel great contentment.

NOTES

1. Unpublished study showing results of women and work survey, *Today's Christian Woman*, July/Aug. 1991, 2.
2. W. E. Vine, *Vine's Expository Dictionary of Old & New Testament Words* (Old Tappan, N.J.: Revell, 1981).
3. Ibid.

· · · · · · · · · · · · ·

How lovely is your dwelling place, O Lord Almighty!

My soul yearns, even faints for the courts of the Lord; my heart and my flesh cry out for the living God.

Even the sparrow has found a home, and the swallow a nest for herself, where she may have her young—a place near your altar, O Lord Almighty, my King and my God.

Blessed are those who dwell in your house; they are ever praising you.

Psalm 84:1–4

Chapter Six
. . . .
LONELINESS:
THE FEELING OF
DISCONNECTEDNESS

A vivid picture still hangs in my mind from my little girl days. Our nearest neighbors lived a half mile away. The three Dyer children were our age mates, playmates, and bus-riding companions. Their mother, Virginia, had soft curly brown hair and kind, large eyes. I often saw her working beside her husband, her narrow body in farmers' overalls, turning out work like a man. Old Uncle Durb lived with them in their small farm house. This thin, smiling neighbor who laughed and talked at baby showers seemed to have lots of people in her life.

I remember one night I saw her sitting on our kitchen stool, leaning against our round-topped refrigerator, talking earnestly to my mother who was bent over the kitchen sink washing dishes. This never happened in summertime. Day work was long and outside; housework followed after dark. Farm women didn't visit on summer nights. Later I asked Mama why she came.

Mama said she was lonely.

I imagine Virginia now, through my middle-aged mind's eye, returning to her home, walking down our lane, across the field. She would put her hands in her apron pockets, and she would be contented, lonely no more.

LONELINESS OR SOLITUDE?

When are you lonely? Do you know the feeling? Are you lonely in a crowd, in the hustle and bustle of family living, on coffee break at work? Or are you lonely when your world is quiet and no one is around?

Virginia was lonely in her crowded household. People look lonely on elevators when they are inches away from other people, if that. I have looked back during a symphony performance at people who seem to have come alone. One might slump looking dejected as if sad to be alone. Another might lean forward in rapt attention, alone but wrapped in pleasure, music, and the experience of the moment, not lonely at all.

Have you ever treasured moments of total quiet and solitude? I believe that most of us have. Lonely does not really have to do with the world around us, noisy or quiet, people, entertainment.

Loneliness is not a state of outside, it's an inside thing.

I work with teens in a noisy, public high school. Have you ever noticed that pictures of teens usually show them in groups? They are laughing, active, happy to be around each other. However, surveys show that adolescents suffer more from loneliness than any other age group. Seventy-nine percent of teens surveyed said they were sometimes or often lonely. Fifty-three percent of the people in their middle years and only 37 percent of those over fifty-five were lonely.

We often color an older person lonely, with our usual picture being that of a woman sitting in her comfy chair with no one to share her hours. In real life, as people get older, the opposite is often true. They adjust. In fact, older women who are alone are more content than older men.

We also color the single woman as the most lonely. This too is a myth. According to recent surveys, married women are as likely to be lonely as single women. Some surveys indicate married women are more lonely.

I have a good friend who has been single for fifteen years. She is not lonely. In fact, she gets irritated when people assume that because she is single she is dissatisfied. She's not looking for a man. She thrives on making her own decisions, is independent, is self-sufficient, and has some discomfort at another person being in control. If she were married, I can imagine her struggling to fit her pace to someone else's living style—and feeling lonely inside.

My friend and I were in Hawaii and decided to drive to a small town called Hana. The road clings tortuously to the side of the mountain, with hair-pin turns on hills meandering along the ocean's edge. My friend wanted to drive to Hana and back. Most would consider this white-knuckle drive an endurance test to be shared equally with her companion. Not my friend! Between the way God created her and her lifetime experiences, she is happy to be in control of her circumstances—even seven hours of miserable driving conditions made more exciting by the bizarre driving behavior of the cars in front of us.

I learned a new lesson on our trip to Hana. I tell it to you as a growth possibility in your friendships also. As two Christian women, sisters by adoption in God's family, we are quite different, though we also have strong similarities. My assumptions had been off target. Lonely to her is *not* what is lonely to me. I needed to give her room to be different, to not assume her needs are the same as mine. I have a sneaking suspicion this is true in other women's lives and between other sisters.

Our Hana drive taught me to accept my friend's different needs and personality. Women, we will never break down barriers of loneliness that separate us until we allow each other to be real. Real and different.

When my children were small, I yearned for an older friend who would be my spiritual mentor. A vivacious Christian woman moved to our neighborhood. I thought my instructor/friend had arrived. But she did not become my spiritual mentor in the way I expected. At that stage in our lives, we made a great entertainment team, and she rescued me more than once by caring for my children to give me breathing room.

God gave her the delightful ability to always see positives in my children, laugh, and take the world lightly. While this was not the description of "mentor" I had told God I needed, she was precisely what He knew I needed most.

In the decade of our friendship, she has set an example for me of adaptability in reentering the job market, accepting the people her children married, reminding me of each of my children's charm when I find them uncharming, and a host of other examples I needed—while being fun.

Had I abandoned the relationship because it did not match my expectations for what I needed, I would have lost a precious friendship.

Mixed Messages

Women get mixed messages about loneliness today. If we read the headlines of popular women's magazines, having a man around is supposed to help women feel complete. But then, we also hear messages that independence is bliss—if you're somebody, you need *nobody*.

As a Christian, it rather irks me that feminists distort the message that a woman is complete without a man. God actually made us as separate persons and is the One who provides ultimate satisfaction to the woman who chooses not to marry. This is a Christian truth, not a secular feminist innovation.

Married women, whether Christian or not, may feel quite alone in the world. Having a man to go home to is not the answer to a woman's loneliness. If only secular feminists speak out on this issue, women will be misled. *Christian women* need to address this issue. People who struggle need straight answers.

Discussion from Christian women about loneliness could help prevent divorce and lesbianism, to name two important issues that have been affected by the silence of Christian women. I include myself among the silent. I should have said more.

People in my profession define loneliness as a state of mental pain or anguish caused by feelings of separation or feelings of nothingness. From this definition we can see why married women feel loneliness as frequently as single women do.

The simple statistic that up to half of all marriages end in divorce tells us that many married women are not content enough in their marriages to stay married. And some who are content find themselves single by their husbands' choice. What was contentment for the women was not for their mates.

Although surveys tell us different things about which married women are lonely and why, we know that a marriage license does not guarantee a sense of connection and inner feeling of completeness.

A recent best-seller, *The Erotic Silence of the American Wife*, written by Dalma Heyn, tells us that more wives are having affairs at an earlier age. Loneliness may be a factor, but so might our culture's easy acceptance of outside sexual relationships or a host of other reasons.

Loneliness in women may be connected to:

employment

    whether she works outside her home

    whether she finds companionship in her work

    whether her work is isolating

    whether her work is satisfying

volunteerism

    spending time with others in churches,

    clubs, political groups, or shared missions

relationships

    whether she lives alone

    the goodness of fit in relationships with those

    important to her

life stage, not age

    a young mother with three preschoolers may be quite

    lonely while her age mate without children

    might be satisfied by adult friendships

health
    older women's loneliness is often affected by
    deteriorating health that brings isolation
self-acceptance
    a woman who likes her own company is less likely to
    feel lonely when she is alone

"She is her own worst enemy" is a truth with a parallel.
You can be your own best friend.

Somehow that sounds impossible—but it's not. It simply means you like your own company because you like who you are.

Is the emotion of loneliness different for women than men? I'm sure it is. We said earlier that loneliness is not an outside thing, it is an inside matter. Women who are single get a different message from our culture than men do. Stereotypically, if a woman is single, she is unhappy, missing something. A single man is considered "free." If a single woman takes this message inside, she will feel, and the feeling won't be good. The outside message sets up an inside expectation.

Why Do We Feel Lonely?

Why are we lonely? Because we expect something different from what we have. As women, if we are lonely and single, we may not have expected to be single at this time in our lives. If we are lonely and married, we did not expect our marriage relationship to be what it is.

Expectations: an inside thing.

There is a difference between loneliness, aloneness, and solitude. When do you welcome being alone? When do you fear being alone? Think of a friend or perhaps a sister if you have one. Are her happy alone spaces the same as yours?

When do you welcome solitude? How much solitude do you hunger for? I have three sisters with whom I share a wonderful, strange bond which we call the "sisterhood," but we have each discovered that we have *large* needs for solitude. In fact, we're in trouble when we "people" too much. Some of you know this feeling.

If you don't know the feeling, that's fine. It's not a matter of normal or weird, happy or sad, just different. Although the need may begin with how we have been created by our Maker, life experiences polish, refine, and shape us.

Perhaps you don't see people often enough, or at least your contacts are limited to more casual encounters rather than intimate friendships. Join a group, volunteer, or attend a class for people with the same interests as you. That can put you with a number of people you have potential to "click" with. If you don't seem to make friends in the group after you've been there a while, you might want to ask somebody what your body language and actions are communicating: Are you unintentionally projecting a request for distance, or are you trying so hard to make friends that people are a bit intimidated by you?

I wonder if Esther felt lonely as an orphan taken in by her cousin Mordecai? Did she remember her parents' death? Did she feel lonely when she entered King Xerxes's palace to be pampered for a year, getting ready to take her chance at being queen? She could have felt used, but I doubt it. My guess is that her attitude kept her from staying lonely.

Surely she felt it; she couldn't reveal her nationality, she could not speak of her roots. She experienced no sisterhood in the palace. And after she became queen, do you imagine King Xerxes to be her one and only? Her "what a man" companion? I hardly think so. As a young virgin she married an old man with a harem, a Jewish girl and a Gentile king. Esther was incredible at adapting. Her Creator, when He fashioned her in her mother's womb, knew every day of her life ahead. The code on each of her cells carried the preparation for adventure. Each day of her childhood shaped and refined her potential as she approached her life in the palace.

Loneliness was surely an emotion that could have forced her to escape back to her cousin, back to her people. But she chose to experience loneliness without allowing bitterness to creep into her soul. Did she have to battle feelings of being a nonentity in her lonely moments? I don't know. Possibly she did. If so, she won. We know because she stayed where she could have been lonely but there accomplished her mission.

It seems to me that loneliness is a positive or negative emotion depending on a woman's choice, not her circumstances. *Loneliness is a choice, our decision in our circumstances.* Although we may not choose life circumstances which make us alone, we may choose our feelings when we are alone.

I wish that in this decade we could break down the barriers that define loneliness as a condition determined by being married or single. I believe this would be a victory for unity among women. There is so much more to unity than shared marital status.

The apostle Paul talks about choosing to marry or not to marry without referring to gender (1 Corinthians 7). Either women or men may make that choice. My daughter now says she doesn't think she's called to be a "Pauline creature." Twenty-three and single, her stirrings involve other people in her future. But that expectation may change. I wish to communicate to her that she is ever my daughter and fully accepted whether she remains single or marries.

We know that God creates us with differences. It is realistic that He would create some of us to thrive being single and others being married. My wish would be that each woman be free to choose as her Creator leads.

Studies show that women who are single by choice or circumstance thrive on freedom, independence, opportunities to develop friendships, and the search for personal development. Their freedom allows them to take advantage of the exceptional opportunities in our world today: travel, work, career moves, quests that become more complicated when married, and other quests that become challenging mountains for those who have also chosen parenthood. Christian women who are single often find they have more time for ministry than they would if married. Their freedom allows a dimension in ministry different from a woman who is married. (I speak as a seasoned, married-with-four-children person, who also desires to minister!)

We can choose to respect our sisters' freedom rather than envy it. We can choose to cooperate, to see how we can work *together* with other women. For a single woman with extra time or money, that might mean baby-sitting for a family who can't afford to pay a baby-sitter, sending an anonymous food or financial gift to a needy family in the church, or just being flexible when a married friend's schedule changes suddenly when you were supposed to do something together. For a married woman, cooperation means keeping up college friendships with individuals who have stayed single, realizing that some single people in the church approach the holidays hoping desperately that somebody will invite them over for dinner, and staying up-to-date on subjects other than husbands and diapers. For all women, it means looking at what we have in common rather than assuming life differences make understanding impossible.

And we can choose to live our mission in our circumstances rather than complaining and whining—both to God and others. I confess to being guilty of both. I have envied single women's freedom and complained to both God and my husband about my encumbrances.

I remember being ten months pregnant with our third child. (My doctor said this is impossible. I still believe it, and *know* I felt ten months pregnant.) I had gained sixty pounds and was less than comfortable. Venturing to downtown Chicago, I met a friend for lunch. Afterward we toured her apartment on Walton Street and she showed me her newly designed kitchen complete with a view of Lake Michigan. I'm sure she weighed half as much as I did and her life was twice as exciting. She was excited about praying for the city, was ministering in her church, and her calendar was full of events to look forward to.

I lumbered home lonely.

Have you experienced moments like that—where you could choose to stay lonely, become bitter, or see the positives in your circumstances?

CHOICES FOR LONELY PEOPLE

Sometimes we can change our circumstances and sometimes we cannot. Let's assume that we either cannot or choose not to. If the circumstances are given, we have three positive possibilities.

We can accept.

We can adapt.

We can create.

Accept

The "Serenity Prayer" speaks powerfully to our feeling of lone-liness: "God grant me the serenity to accept the things I cannot change; the courage to change the things I can; and the wisdom to know the difference."

When circumstances of life equal loneliness, as in Esther's life, women who are isolated for health or other reasons, or a host of other life events, our only choice may be to accept. The unchange-able can be accepted with a God-focus that refuses to be defeated and negative. Or the unchangeable can be accepted as motivation for whining, griping, and general misery.

While no other woman can tell you *how* you can adapt, we can share ideas.

Adapt

Give up your expectations for relationship.
No friend will be the perfect companion.
No husband will meet all your needs.
No child will fulfill all your dreams.
God alone promises to meet *all* our needs, but He doesn't promise to do so in the here and now.

Create

No other woman can tell you how to create contentment from your loneliness, but we can share ideas.

1. Create a support network.

What do you need? What appropriate ways can you satisfy this need?

Give yourself permission to look for new friends.

Give yourself permission to have a few close friends rather than many superficial friendships (even if you are the pastor's wife and some may think you have favorites). Jesus set this example.

2. Create a positive sense of esteem for yourself.

One of the ways to raise self-esteem is by risk-taking. Nothing succeeds like success, even if interspersed with failure. My many manuscript rejections do not overshadow the one yes that means I can communicate with a woman I'll never meet.

3. Create in solitude.

Solitude can be enjoyable if you do not fear experimenting. I experiment with words. My sister Nadine experiments with painting scenes from nature. Some read and travel through the pages creating mental images of places they've been from their reading chair. Create music, clothing, creations of cuisine, whatever satisfies the solitude in your soul.

4. Create a more intimate relationship with your Creator.

You will find this process to be a lifetime of stimulation. The paradox of friendship with our Creator, companionship with One with whom it is unnecessary to explain "Why" will be the high point of your life.

5. Create close friendships from casual relationships.

Suppose you have chosen to deepen your friendships. "She who would have friends will prove herself to be one."

But how? Any bookstore has books, manuals, and guides for making friends. I think the book of Proverbs is the best. Solomon's advice about making friends and keeping them is relevant today. He said wise things because his Creator was speaking through him. Here's a small sample in my own words.

Listen selectively. Gossip hurts friendships (Proverbs 16:28).

Forgive, forget, and keep confidences (Proverbs 17:9).

Acquaintances and soul sisters are different. A soul sister shares your goals (Proverbs 18:24). Note: A woman of many friends (Hebrew—neighbor/acquaintance) comes to ruin, but there is a friend (Hebrew—one who loves, shares goals) who sticks closer than a sister.

The best friends are those whose motives are pure (Proverbs 22:11).

Don't overstay your welcome. (Know your friends' solitude needs!) (Proverbs 25:17). Ben Franklin said fish and house guests stink in three days.

Saying "Cheer up" when someone is hurting hurts (Proverbs 25:20).

Be sensitive to your friend's personal schedule (Proverbs 27:14).

Be real. Shared differences can make you both richer (Proverbs 27:17).

Sexual liaisons without marriage will get you trouble, not friendship (Proverbs 6:32).

When you have power to act and accomplish something good, just do it (Proverbs 3:27).

Simple love is better than glamorous hate (Proverbs 15:17).

Solomon, for all his wisdom, had the same problem we have. He *knew* more than he was able to *live*.

Let's say you would like to develop a close, transparent friendship. How do you begin? Make a list of several people you would like to get to know better. Ask God to help you mature as you develop relationships that honor Him. Select one or two for special attention based on the following criteria:

1. Is this woman a Christian? The common bond of the Holy Spirit is essential for this kind of relationship.

2. Do you respect and trust this person, based on what you know?

3. Do you have enough differences to be stimulating to each other?

Take time to get to know this person. Call her and invite her to have breakfast or lunch with you. Initially it may be good to meet in a restaurant where you can concentrate on each other rather than on household distractions. Become acquainted with her family, and introduce her to yours. If you are both married, don't expect your husbands to establish friendships; transparent foursomes are rare. Remember that your children may not be fond of each other either. Those are not criteria for your relationship, just as marital status is not.

Discover how you can practice friendly thoughtfulness. Does she like plants, butterflies, shopping at flea markets? An occasional card will show her you are thinking of her. Drop by—briefly—with something from your kitchen when her schedule is full. Do fun things together. Garden, repot houseplants, go garage-sale bingeing. Rigid routines are not the stuff friendships are made of.

How do you have time for each other? Few people have spare time. Two friends with eleven children between them found they could seldom get together. They both saved their kitchen cleanup until their children had gone to school on Friday morning. One called the other. With long telephone cords, they washed and wiped, started supper, baked, and scrubbed as they talked.

There are disappointments in friendships. Perhaps you discover that the person you thought would be your closest companion doesn't work out. Enjoy what profit there has been in the relationship. Give your expectation to God and remember that He is not unaware of your needs.

If God had created us all alike, would we ever be lonely? I think not. Someone else could know exactly how we feel. But "human" means no one else has your fingerprints, no one else creates an identical footprint in the sand. Perhaps when we feel lonely we can accept that feeling as a reminder that we are created uniquely in His image—which is better than being like any other human!

STEPS TO TAKE

1. What realistic changes can I make in my circumstances regarding my loneliness?

2. What choices can I make in my attitude in circumstances I cannot change?

3. Do I have an inner circle of friends with whom I can share my inmost feelings (if you identify this as a need in your life)?

4. How can I nurture those friendships that I wish to be stronger? Reorder priority time commitments to share experiences. Learn biblical principles to be a better friend.

5. Give your expectations of relationship to God.

· · · · · · · · · · · · ·

Blessed is the [woman] who does not walk in the counsel of the wicked or stand in the way of sinners or sit in the seat of mockers.

But [her] delight is in the law of the Lord, and on his law [she]
meditates day and night.

[She] is like a tree planted by streams of water, which yields its
fruit in season and whose leaf does not wither. Whatever
[she] does prospers.

Psalm 1:1–3

May those who hope in you not be disgraced because of me, O
Lord, the Lord Almighty; may those who seek you not be put
to shame because of me, O God of Israel.

Psalm 69:6

Chapter Seven

LOVE:
THE MARK OF
GOD'S WOMAN

A television program once featured impersonators. After the performances, the question was asked, "Will the real Miss Smith please stand up?" Did you ever try to guess the *real* person? I found it hard to pick the truth-teller.

How do you tell a Christian woman from one who is not? Is there any tell-tale difference between a woman who is *connected* to her Creator and one who is *detached* from the One who gave her life? Each has a unique personality, mind, and feelings: personalized gifts from the same God.

Can you tell a Christian by her dress code, a piece of jewelry, a membership card, her facial expression, address, marital status, number of children, job, what's printed on her business card?

The mark of a Christian woman is love. Her love is different from other women's love.

Knowing this automatically establishes one given: The evil one who wants Christians to immobilize, downsize, and paralyze will twist it and put his own spin on love.

He's doing pretty well, don't you think? Most movies portray love as sex. Some song lyrics mix love and sheer madness. Finding real examples of people marked with honest-to-God love is a challenging search.

I think of two friends, Katie and Margaret, who seem to love easily. Their love gives, forgives, includes, exudes, carries them and others through tough times. Some women have the mark. Some of us struggle, as I do, most of the time.

Love is internal. "But now these three remain: faith, hope and love. But the greatest of these is love" (1 Corinthians 13:13). It's also external. John teaches us that if we say we are Christians, but don't act like it, we're not. "Dear [women], let us not love with words or tongue but with actions and in truth" (1 John 3:18). Direct teaching, isn't it? Love is our test as well as our mark.

God is love. Love originated with Him. Without Him, love has one simple result; it will end. We can use the word; we can clang the cymbals; we can splash it on billboards; we can sing of it and dance to its lyrics. But love will be gone. And that's what has happened.

The Bible has been closed. Man and woman—beings who began with dust and will end the same way—have said, "We will write the definition. We will make the rules." And love has gone. In its place warm feelings may linger, but they will eventually grow cold. In its place may be marriage licenses, but they will be dissolved by the courts. In its place a "love child" may be born, but that child will be branded illegitimate and may never know one of his parents. In its place church steeples may be built, with bells pealing and light gleaming through stained glass windows, but bickering, gossip, envy, and doubt will remain within.

LOVE MYTHS

I have been tainted by love myths. Some are especially appealing to women and as devastating as they are appealing. Like the extraordinary piece of fruit in Eve's garden, love myths are poisonous.

LOVE

. . . . .

Myths and the Truth About Love

We fall in love.	**Love is an act of the will.** (Falling is accidental. Should our greatest source of power and comfort be determined by an accident?)
Love is beyond our control.	**Love has boundaries.** (Jesus modeled love boundaries.)
Living with a man unmarried is a test of love.	**Sex is only appropriate within the covenant of marriage.** (Couples who marry after living together have a higher divorce rate.)
Love is only a feeling.	**Love is feeling and much more.** (Love is power—our greatest power since we are God's image bearers. Love is a command requiring response whether or not we feel love at the moment.)
Love justifies hurtful, mindless action.	**True love is putting the other person first, not just feeling emotions for him or her.** (All is *not* fair in love and war, even though we use the excuse.)

What is the solution? We must teach our children that they will *select* their lifetime mates. First, the husband or wife must be a Christian. The Bible says so. Next, his character is more important than his pocketbook or any other feature. Examine his parents. No, the couple will not live with them. But most of the parents' values and characteristics will be combined in their children although they, as in-laws, may be hundreds of miles away.

Myths we are tempted to believe make glamorous movies. They tempt us because they don't hold us accountable as real people with a real tomorrow. Our Creator cares about our tomorrow. He not only tells us the truth about love, He shows us through stories in Scripture how to love.

Love Stories

There is no love without sacrifice. And sacrifice looks to the future at the expense of the present. A husband sacrifices to provide for his family. He feels like sinking into the easy chair with newspaper and earplugs in place. Instead, he romps with the children and fixes a clogged drain. A mother aches for a full night's sleep, but her infant rouses her, needing to be nursed. A frightened child needs to be rocked and soothed. Our mate is experiencing stress; fatigue has wiped the smile from her face or the ruddy color from his cheek. We sacrifice. We expend energy to take up the slack and lighten the load. We spend minutes fixing his favorite spiced tea, cheering him when we're weary ourselves. Yes, love demands. Love is a complex combination of our minds, our wills, and our emotions. Love requires our feet, our hands, and our feelings. The emotion that will not sacrifice is not love.

Great love stories often come from unlikely circumstances. I personalize the story of the Good Samaritan and create a mental current video. I visualize the people as women, which takes a bit of imagination and a trans-century mind set, but it's a beautiful love story.

A woman travels a path of risks. It's an errand that is necessary, and risks must be taken. She is jumped, robbed, and left to die.

A select group of women are to be the caretakers of the needy. But the organization has grown, and their policies multiply—for everyone's good, of course. One of the group's members walks by the woman in distress. She would violate a policy by helping her sister. She passes by on the far side.

Another woman passes by. She's not in "the organization." It's not her job to help. In fact, she'll be delayed on her own trip, and she doesn't know for sure what the woman's need is. Furthermore, she might get mugged herself; then what good could she be for anyone? Maybe there's a phone ahead. She'll dial 911 and be a conscientious informer. She passes by a bit nearer.

Another woman comes along. She's not a member of "the organization" and cannot access its resources to help this woman. Never mind. She has her own shawl, oil of Vitamin E, a little wine, and some bandages in her travel case. She gently helps her sister into her car and takes her to a woman's crisis center, pays for medical help, and says, "I can help more, if needed. I'll be back."

Which woman loved? Which was the marked woman?

Another unlikely love story involves a man and his first and second wives. This is not a story of marital bonding, but rather a higher love.

King Xerxes was married to Queen Vashti. (What names!) At the time, important men's wives were chosen based on beauty. (Of course, we've come a long way today from such superficial measures.) Queens were accessories.

King Xerxes gave a 180-day power parade followed by a seven-day bash, or rather banquet. After seven days of drinking, King Xerxes had a bright idea. He would treat his guests to a special viewing of his wife.

She said no.

Now, from what I've read in the commentaries, my view of her response is unique. (I haven't found a commentary written by a woman.) I believe no was an appropriate answer. Was displaying one's wife at a drunken party an act of respect? Was unchecked power a godly source of unity in marriage? She had no need or desire to be displayed.

Of course, King Xerxes was angry, and embarrassed, no doubt. Some power he had! I chuckle to imagine the response of his wise advisers. "Wait till the guys hear this. There will be disrespect and discord in all the nobles' households. We've got to nip this in the bud."

I hope to discuss these things with Queen Vashti if I meet her in heaven. I imagine she delighted in the solitude that was her punishment for saying no.

Vashti's answer became an open door for another woman of principle to enter King X's life. But Esther did not beome his wife based on her character, but on having the good fortune to win the king's special beauty contest.

Due to Haman's conspiracy and hunger for power, King X made another foolish decision. He signed the order that his people kill all the Jews in his country. Esther being Jewish was at risk (although the king did not know her ancestry), but she also had power. She was his wife.

Based on her love for her people, and her love and respect for her adoptive father, she approached the king uninvited. This was illegal even for wives. She caught his attention in her finery. Iron-ic? a senseless risk? a trivial technique? I see that I should be careful in judging. We cannot see other women's hearts or know their motivation.

Her action saved her people. No doubt she acted in fear. Her heart might have been telling her to run away as Hagar did—and Jonah, and Elijah. But she stood—waiting the king's motion of acceptance or doom.

"If I perish, I perish."

Her words have encouraged me through many of my baby steps of faith.

She acted on a higher love.

Let's take the principles of these love stories and apply them specifically to myths that tempt us. Since I like to learn through pictures, I visualize love myths as being like sand castles.

Sand Castle Love

As children we used to sing a song about a wise man who built his house on a rock and a foolish man who built his dwelling on the sand.

I think women today are tempted to build sand castle love. We are so bombarded by the messages of human love that higher love is crowded out. When the power of love moves us and we confuse these two loves, we are vulnerable to the emotional wipeout of a tidal wave. Have you ever found yourself living in these sand castles?

The following myths are examples of sand castle love. We give our soul, body, money (if we have any), and energy to the building project, and then we move in.

- Love means giving ourselves away without boundaries. ("She can't help herself. She's in love.")
- Love justifies marrying someone who is not a Christian.
- Sexual satisfaction is enough to carry us through any adversity or crisis.
- Love with one hand on the doorknob for escape will keep love fresh. (Try fragile, fading, and gone.)

- True love will always be pleasant and exciting.
- Sexual intimacy and love are the same emotion.
- Taking physical abuse is acceptable because we're in love.
- Emotional control is justified because we're loved.

Those of us who have a few years of living behind us are learning what happens to sand castle love when the facts of life roll in. Like the foolish man's house, the relationship goes FLOP! The principles of higher love are described in Scripture. Since human love and higher love may feel similar, here are some ways to distinguish the two.

HUMAN LOVE	HIGHER LOVE
love between humans: woman and friend, husband, or child	love between a person and God
love confined to specific circumstances	flexible, expanding love that lasts through changes
love that requires a return	covenant, one-way love
external security— this person makes me feel good	internal security—gives the appearance of independence— actually is God-dependent

Real living is not as simple as the chart on the next page, but it helps me understand love in relationships. Being Christians does not mean we can love other people like we love God. Although we can give unconditional love to God, we cannot give unconditional love without boundaries to people. One of my toughest life-lessons in love is realizing that boundaries must exist. Others may or may not set them.

God approves boundary setting. He sets boundaries for His people. Jesus lived as a human being setting boundaries. They guide and give me examples for learning so that I can set boundaries in my relationships.

I think women have a harder time learning this lesson. Our Christian subculture has expected women to live with inappropriate boundaries, such as when pastors have advised women to

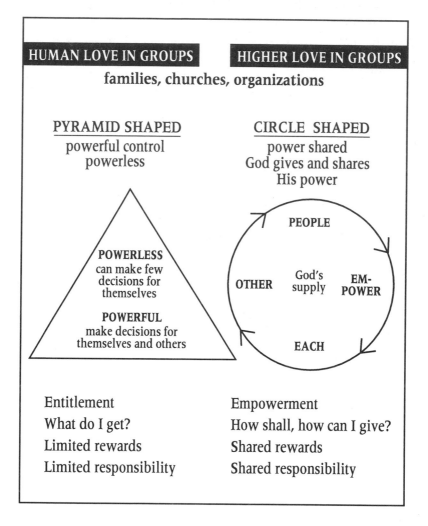

HUMAN LOVE IN GROUPS   HIGHER LOVE IN GROUPS
families, churches, organizations

PYRAMID SHAPED
powerful control
powerless

CIRCLE SHAPED
power shared
God gives and shares
His power

PEOPLE

POWERLESS
can make few
decisions for
themselves

OTHER   God's
supply   EM-
POWER

POWERFUL
make decisions for
themselves and others

EACH

Entitlement
What do I get?
Limited rewards
Limited responsibility

Empowerment
How shall, how can I give?
Shared rewards
Shared responsibility

stay with abusive husbands. Most women who were abused as children struggle with setting their own boundaries as well as respecting others' boundaries.

I can give my unconditional love to God because I can trust Him. How do I know that's impossible with people? By looking in the mirror! Being a ceramic pot on clay feet instead of a golden vase on a brass pedestal, if a person loves me no matter what, I will take advantage of the person! At least I'll be tempted to.

Our two stories, those of Esther and the Good Samaritaness, show us that there are times when we love with a higher love in human relationships. Giving with no guarantees and sacrificing may be loving on solid ground—if our greatest Lover directs us to do so. He gives us strength for standing, or giving—saying no with secure boundaries, or yes with the power of love.

Sexuality: Our Culture's Substitute for Love

A coworker and I were talking in my office. He asked me to go on a trip with him. He described what we could see and do together. He was married; I was and still am married. What he was suggesting would have violated his promises to his wife and my promises to my husband.

I said no.

"Every woman can be had for a price," he answered. "What's yours?"

I remembered a line from Kitty, the bartending beauty from "Gunsmoke." (She's not my spiritual heroine, but she had a few lines that describe real life at its less-than-best.) In her country drawl, she said, "I never met a man who didn't think he knew all there was to know about women."

I smiled realizing I had met one of those men.

I have been inspired by noble, godly women to say some profound things. This was not one of those times, nor one of those lines.

"I do have my price, and it's out of your reach."

Christian women are tempted. What makes the difference between standing strong or going down? I think the answer is the same for single and married women. We stand strong when we believe we have a price. It is so incredibly high that only our Creator could pay it. Because we are Christians our total being is purchased by God—at the very large expense of His Son.

We have two choices: marriage with monogamous sexuality or singleness with celibacy.

Either of those choices is not always fun or satisfying and without cost and sacrifice. If you talk with a group of honest women, you'll find in either category there are those who wish they'd made different choices. Christian women today are also tempted to find satisfaction in homosexual relationships. You and I should not be surprised when temptation comes, no matter how strange it seems. Scripture tells us that no temptation has come to any woman that has not been faced by women before. And God will provide a way of escape.

I talked with a small group of girls where I work. The topic was pregnancy and staying in school. Their talk ranged from literal fights girls have over boys to when and why they might go to bed with a boy. "How much love does it take to get to you? I mean, you can't hold out forever!" This fourteen-year-old girl and her friends giggled. I stuck to my calling of being salt in a public school. We talked about consequences, abstinence, commitment. The bell rang too soon.

As I walked back to my little office, this young girl's question reminded me of my covenant commitment to God regarding sexuality.

"God, I can't believe You kept loving me when I didn't love You back. And then I became a Christian. And You keep loving me no matter what."

It doesn't matter how much love it takes for God to get to you as far as He is concerned. He'll never give up.

Let's assume that I wanted to convince you that it was for your good and you would be happier if: given that you are married, you are sexually faithful, OR given that you are single, you are celibate. How could I convince you?

From the figures in my counseling office, I could give you statistics on sexually transmitted diseases, the failure rate of condoms, medical information about AIDS, and the consequences of unplanned pregnancy. I know that, sobering as these facts are, they have not changed the behavior of teen girls including Christian girls. I don't know whether information is more convincing for more mature women. I do know that the power of loving God is the greatest power I have ever experienced. I do know that loving God is the greatest motivator in my life.

I believe that *nothing less than His love* can give us the courage to say no. No other love will motivate us to find the escape door. Our world is saturated with opportunities to be unfaithful. Our world's approval of any immoral lifestyle, whether heterosexual or homosexual, is moving from disapproval to a magnetic force.

- Impressive statistics on the value of abstinence,
- Fear of consequences, physical as well as emotional,
- Sexual health risks as deadly as Russian roulette, or
- Even another incredible, lovable human:

All these can be erased from our mind by the evil one. All these can seem trivial. All these can be rationalized to zero.

I believe that *nothing less than His forgiveness* can give us the courage to say no after we've said yes to the wrong person at the wrong time.

No matter what we have done in the past, it is never too late to make a covenant with our Creator. "I ask forgiveness for not living by your guidelines for sexuality. I commit my sexuality to You, God, to follow your instructions, because I love You, and You are God."

In our rapidly changing world, no matter how dark or bleak, the mark of God's woman will distinguish her. God's higher love not only lifts us; He gives His power to live as women distinguished by the mark.

STEPS TO TAKE

1. Plan for permanence. Though you cannot control any relationship, plan to love for a lifetime.

2. Which of the relationships in your life need to be fortified with love?

3. Think of the story of the Good Samaritan. Does a needy person come to your mind? How might you serve that person with a higher love?

4. List characteristics about a person you admire whose life is marked by love. What characteristics did your Creator make in you so that you can mirror His love?

5. Make a plan to communicate love to one person. Only you can make the plan. Take your mother-in-law out to lunch on your husband's birthday. It was a special day for her too! Tell your teenager what characteristics you like in her/him. Give your friend a time check. That person can fill in the blank with where you go together and what you do.

6. Ask God to remind you during ordinary living that you carry His mark.

· · · · · · · · · · · · ·

If you make the Most High your dwelling—even the Lord, who is my refuge—then no harm will befall you, no disaster will come near your tent.

For he will command his angels concerning you to guard you in all your ways; they will lift you up in their hands, so that you will not strike your foot against a stone.

You will tread upon the lion and the cobra; you will trample the great lion and the serpent.

"Because [she] loves me," says the Lord, "I will rescue [her]; I will protect [her], for [she] acknowledges my name.

[She] will call upon me, and I will answer [her]; I will be with [her] in trouble, I will deliver [her] and honor [her].

With long life will I satisfy [her] and show [her] my salvation."

Psalm 91:9–16

Chapter Eight

ANXIETY (WORRY): THE BACKPACK OF STRESS, STRAIN, AND SIGNIFICANCE

Oops! This emotion is neither good nor God-given. God gives us the emotion of *concern*, the feeling of *caring*. But anxiety is "concern" gone amok. Our instruction Book tells us not to be anxious about anything (Philippians 4:6).

We will be ineffective Christians when we no longer care about our world or ourselves. Our Creator does not want our feeling of caring squelched. But anxiety is not God-given concern. Anxiety is an octopus that magnifies our concerns, tangles them in feelings of powerlessness, and can immobilize us.

Worry is a socially acceptable emotion in many of us, even among our Christian friends and acquaintances. We worry about healthcare, investments, and whether social security will support us in later years. We worry about church politics, our relatives' financial status, and our reputations. We worry about our appearance and what our kids are doing.

Sometimes our anxieties catapult us from the frying pan to the fire. If we are anxious about living alone, we can jump into a mismatched marriage. Girls tell me in my counseling office that they have intercourse in order to keep their boyfriends. Their anxiety about security in relationships results in hurt and disgust with themselves, and it does not secure the relationship. I groan inside remembering that my generation did the same thing. I wish for better choices for girls today.

Reading Scripture, I see that King Saul was worried that Priest Samuel would not get to the sacrifice program on time. So he offered the sacrifices—which was not in his job description (1 Samuel 13:8–14).

Abraham and Hagar conceived Ishmael because Sarah thought God's time clock was running out for making a baby. Centuries of war and rivers of blood later, the truth is God doesn't have to follow any clock. Time is His invention, not His master.

Webster says anxiety is painful uneasiness of mind over an impending or anticipated ill. It is being disquieted over an impending or unknown future event.

WHY WE FEEL IT

Certainly our world today provides lots of opportunity for anxiety. Have you ever noticed that if you allow your mind to begin worrying, it wants to binge? Like rabbits, worry is a prolific reproducer.

Jesus tells a story that describes different people. In His graphic way, He shows us worry, why we feel it, and its product.

> Hear then the parable of the sower. When anyone hears the word of the kingdom, and does not understand it, the evil one comes and snatches away what has been sown in [her] heart. This is the one on whom seed was sown beside the road. And the one on whom seed was sown on the rocky places, this is the [woman] who hears the word, and immediately receives it with joy; yet [she] has no firm root in [herself], but is only temporary, and when affliction or persecution arises because of the word, immediately [she] falls away.

Most commentaries agree that the above two illustrations are people who do not accept God as their Creator.

And the one on whom seed was sown among the thorns, this is the [woman] who hears the word, and the worry of the world, and the deceitfulness of riches choke the word, and it becomes unfruitful. And the one on whom seed was sown on the good soil, this is the [woman] who hears the word and understands it; who indeed bears fruit, and brings forth, some a hundredfold, some sixty, and some thirty. (Matthew 13:18–23)

Four kinds of women are described here. The first two are not Christians. The last two are. But the two Christians are as different as ice and fire. One was a low-to-no impact person for her Creator's kingdom. The other made a difference. One's life was choked by worries, riches, and pleasures. She never matured. The other soaked in the Word, never gave up, and produced a harvest.

Worry is a thief. It cannot steal our ultimate position of living with Jesus after this life. But it can steal our peace and contentment. Worry keeps us from being productive in ordinary living; we produce no spiritual fruit. Worry ravages the present and stalks our future.

The bottom line for worry is this: Do I believe God will meet my needs? Am I afraid He'll put some of my "needs" in the "wants" category?

When you struggle with worry, let these promises roll over your mind:

- Do not be anxious about anything, but in everything, by prayer and petition, with thanksgiving, present your requests to God. And the peace of God, which transcends all understanding, will guard your hearts and your minds in Christ Jesus. (Philippians 4:6–7)
- And my God will meet all your needs according to his glorious riches in Christ Jesus. (Philippians 4:19)
- Do not worry about your life, what you will eat; or about your body, what you will wear. Life is more than food, and the body more than clothes. (Luke 12:22–23)

People in Jesus' day worried about the same things we do: unpaid bills, security for the future, food, wardrobes, and dying. When Jesus told them not to worry about their "life," I believe their "life" worries paralleled ours: reputation, personal significance, people's expectations, and career paths. Scripture doesn't use those words, but stories like the rich young ruler (Mark 10:17–31) and the vineyard owner (Matthew 21:33–46) describe our temptations.

He promises to give us the desires of our heart, a fact we remember easily. But He asks us first to delight in Him. He asks us to look for His kingdom—and then He will add what we need for the search (Luke 12:31). Our needs are simple: air, food, water, stimulation, love, self-worth, reproduction (unless we are called to celibacy), power, comfort, and security. His world has the potential to supply every physical need. Emotional needs can be met through relationships—the body of believers, marriage, families, community. Caring for the earth and making it productive and beautiful satisfies our needs for power, self-worth, and security.

But the world turned. And we humans decided to meet our needs without God. As a result, there is plenty in parts of the earth and starvation in others. People live in families, work surrounded by people, crowd into commuter trains, and feel lonely twenty-four hours a day. Power becomes a tool to control others rather than to serve. Politics become pathetic and laws become powerless.

Let's create a mental picture together. Picture you and me as two travelers in a different country. We are wearing backpacks. Our Creator will fill our backpacks with what we need. However, we decide we would rather pack for ourselves. I don't know what you would put in your backpack. At different stages in my life, here's what I put in mine (These are my "needs," remember!):

A graduate degree from a Christian institution
Healthy children—no handicaps
Inner confidence based on a secure childhood
Self-esteem based on recognizable accomplishments
No sweating when I'm in front of people
No tears before crowds or with my boss
Just a little more gasoline in my tank which reads E-

I could fill pages with my backpack list. What about you? What's in your backpack? The weight of our expectations get so heavy they weigh us down, choke us.

Sisters, nobody is going to clean out our backpacks for us. Jesus won't grab it and empty the junk. Sometimes other people throw in unnecessary stuff. We have to say no. We have to take responsibility for our own backpacks. We are accountable for what's inside.

As individual women, we make choices. We select what we carry. It is possible for our choices to increase our stress. The normal stress level of life, the healthy balance of satisfaction and challenge, gets bumped up a notch or two. We carry stuff to make us feel significant. Our backpack becomes a real burden. That's usually when I say, "Help, God!"

Churches make choices. The body selects what they will carry as a group of believers. Organizations make choices; nations make choices.

When the world tips out of balance, when people are starving and hurting, then humans look to the heavens and cry, "If there's a god up there, do something! Now that we've ruined the universe, heal it to prove Your existence. Show that You care—our way, not Yours."

DOWNSIZING
OUR BACKPACKS

In a world where evidence of God is often scarce, I see Him clearly when I see women trust Him although they have every human right to worry.

Few women have the "right" to worry as Nada did. Her husband, Ken, had been missing for two days. Her "life" was a fifteen-year challenging marriage commitment, three children, and a job. And, yes, they were both Christians, active in churches where they lived. Ken had served as a board member; they led teen groups and shared the gift of hospitality.

One night Ken didn't come home. What do you tell your ten-year-old son? Her two teenagers kept their usual pace, covering their inner turmoil.

Nada knew there had been a crisis where Ken worked. His twisted face the last time she saw him wasn't characteristic of her husband. She called the company and asked what had happened.

She asked if they knew where he was since he was a frequent business traveler.

"We don't know where he is."

She pleaded for information. "Ask your husband," they said.

But he was gone.

The third morning after he disappeared, Nada wrote, "I give to You, oh Lord, my God, the whereabouts of Kenneth L. Erickson this day, July 14, and I in faith leave him under Your care, knowing that all is well with his soul! Thank You, Lord Jesus, for your comfort this day and for the joy I and the rest of my family can experience, knowing You are in complete charge."

She was drawn to an old garage where Ken and their sixteen-year-old son had been working on an old car. Ken was there. Carbon monoxide had erased the distortion from his face and his life as well.

Nada struggles as a single parent. Needs that were met in her marriage clutch at her like hungry beggars, especially at night. She enters a grocery store where she and Ken used to shop. "Let's get what we have to and get out of here," she says to her son. She feels as though she might round a corner of stacked crackers—and Ken would be there. But he is gone. Like a mirage, he lingers in the spaces they had shared.

Nada and a girlfriend went out to lunch. Men from Ken's company sat at a nearby table. They stared at her. "Do I look that strange?" she whispered to her friend.

Her heart raged. They held secrets. Fear, anger, rage, despair, like thieves, clutched at her peace.

Each child struggled, in his own time, in her own way.

Nada told me that God *met her needs* through it all. God looks pretty big to me through Nada's life. What appears to others as deprivation is not, in this woman's life of faith.

Trusting God

If we have to show God our survival list of needs so He can use it as a handy checklist, He really isn't God; He is a dispense-all programmed by us for us. The truly rich people I know have been through crises that have stripped them. Their lives lack clutter.

Basics like faith and trust are not elusive and ethereal. They live real lives. Their backpacks are not stuffed with junk or even excessive good stuff. The truly rich, if they are materially rich, are not burdened by their wealth. Things do not drive their significance—which levels them with people in poverty.

Nada gave God permission to redefine her needs. Her friends changed, her financial position changed, her social life changed. Her parenting changed. Each child was profoundly affected. She was their Mom, Mom alone.

Today, as I write, she is in the Russian states sharing God as she knows Him. Her children are adults and she has grandchildren. Nada travels light. In my eyes, she's a wealthy woman.

Concern or Worry:
How to Know the Difference

How do we know if we have a valid concern that God intends to use to stimulate us to action? How do we separate concern for those issues from worry about things that distract us from being Christians who make a difference? The Greek word for "anxious" means to be drawn in different directions. What is the difference?

Answering these questions will help you know the difference.

1. Is my concern causing me to serve God better, with more intensity? Does my concern bring glory to God? An unmarried woman can be distracted by her unmet sexual need. Or she can be freed to serve God better by being unmarried (1 Corinthians 7:32–35).

2. Is the concern drawing me to communicate with God more often, more honestly? Or is my "concern" a barrier between God and me, a distraction when I pray? Are my thoughts drawn to the circumstances that confront me rather than to my Creator?

3. Where am I looking for answers? Am I manipulating circumstances to be free of worry? Do I feel I must convince people around me to come around to my way of thinking?

4. Am I experiencing an underlying calm during this time, or are my emotions totally "up for grabs"?

5. What do I expect? Am I just hoping to survive, or am I confidently expecting to come out shining like refined gold?

If my concern is distracting me from being a vibrant Christian, I am worrying. As Christians we have the option when life is tough to plaster on a smile and superficially (through clenched teeth) affirm that we are resting in the Lord. We can worry about the circumstances or get a grip. Getting a grip means we search the Scriptures and live our lives by God's blueprint as we understand it, and as well as we are able. We can allow daily Bible reading to filter through our minds and hearts out to our fingertips and the soles of our feet.

When the tough times come—and you can be sure they will— we *can* get a grip. Our foundation will not be sand; it will be rock solid. God promises that the issues that shake our world are not bigger than or beyond Him. His commitment to us is personal, continual, and inexhaustible. In the crucible of hard times we will not be weighted down with anxiety. We will say with David, "When I said, 'My foot is slipping,' your love, O Lord, supported me. When anxiety was great with me, your consolation brought joy to my soul" (Psalm 94:18–19).

STEPS TO TAKE
1. Determine whether your anxiety comes from an unmet need or want. We may not get what we want; needs are guaranteed.
2. God's intention is not that we violate His Word or nature to "solve" a problem. If your only available action violates His Word, consider doing nothing.
3. Pray about your anxiety. Ask God for peace as well as direction for action.
4. Keep reading Scripture. Often you just "happen" to be reading part of the Word that speaks to your anxiety.
5. Anxiety is the stuff from which the Lord builds faith. When we are out on risk's edge we often feel uncomfortable. But risk's edge is also where faith grows. Peter never would have felt anxiety if he hadn't stepped out of the boat (Matthew 14:25–31). But then he never would have walked on water, either!

ANXIETY (WORRY)

*The Lord reigns, he is robed in majesty; the Lord is robed in
  majesty and is armed with strength. The world is firmly
  established; it cannot be moved.*
Your throne was established long ago; you are from all eternity.
*The seas have lifted up, O Lord, the seas have lifted up their
  voice; the seas have lifted up their pounding waves.*
*Mightier than the thunder of the great waters, mightier than the
  breakers of the sea—the Lord on high is mighty.*
*Your statutes stand firm; holiness adorns your house for endless
  days, O Lord.*

Psalm 93:1–5

Chapter Nine
. . . .
DISCOURAGEMENT:
THE EFFECTS OF
PERCEIVED
FAILURE

*F*ailure. "Lord, I thought You wanted me to do this. I've worked hard. I was sure I had my orders straight from You. Hours of work, hours of my husband being Mr. Mom so I could write. And rejection." I wanted God to examine my past record. "Look at the nights I've spent encouraging other women when my body ached to stay home with a cup of tea. And I've been reading my Bible every day, praying, feeling at peace about what I was doing."

My argument with God about the rejected manuscript was really only the tip of the iceberg. I was discouraged. I was looking for people approval. I was trying to earn position with God. The weight of early years of feeling rejected still kept me from liking what I saw in the mirror. My limited supply of self-esteem was regularly ravaged by the undeniable demands of four growing children.

Hadn't my discipline of scheduling each hour (practically each moment) earned me the right to have a book contract? My children were still clean, involved in lots of activities. My husband continued to board planes for business trips with clean shirts and clean socks. I taught Bible study in our church. (The study preparation, however, was not a discipline—it was my favorite part of the week.)

Well! All that would change now! This living sacrifice was going to slither off the altar.

"I quit."

I wanted a long cry. But there was no time. The pace of life rolled on, but so did my hurt.

ALIBIS FOR HURT

We have lots of options for dealing with our hurts. A workaholic may become a successful seventy-hour-a-week worker in order to avoid stresses at home. Men get more approval for doing this than women do. It's their job, you know. They are just trying to provide for the family. Christians still have not admitted and confronted the insidious worldview that has crowded out family priorities. Christian men can relinquish accountability for family matters. Christian organizations can follow policies that are not family friendly. We give lip service to family values, but frankly little else.

People become churchaholics. Excess in anything helps distract a person who is discouraged.

In my crisis, I found an unlikely comrade. An Egyptian slave named Hagar became special to me. I had always scanned quickly over Genesis 16 before. Why spend time studying a loser? But now I hurt for her. She obeyed her boss, Sarah, followed her orders, and was mistreated. She reacted as I did to discouragement. She ran away.

Our running was different. Hagar was making her way across a desert, perhaps trying to return to Egypt. Being pregnant, this probably was uncomfortable.

My running was camouflaged. Only my husband knew I was quitting. No more writing, speaking, teaching. I would run and remain in my comfortable, carpeted, secure home. Secure from disappointments.

God touched me through Hagar.

"Now the angel of the Lord found her by a spring of water in the wilderness, by the spring on the way to Shur. And he said, 'Hagar, Sarai's maid, where have you come from, and where are you going?'" (Genesis 16:7–8 NASB).

Strange. God knew where she had come from and where she was going. Why did He ask? He asked for Hagar's benefit, not His own.

"Miriam Neff, servant of mine, where have you come from, and where are you going?"

"Lord, I was busy doing Your will. And the results were to be . . ."

"How could you know the results I had planned, daughter? Servants aren't in charge of outcomes. I am not obligated to lay My blueprint before you. In fact, it is for your good that I don't. Why have you been faithful to Me, daughter? Did your confidence in Me get shrink-wrapped in your own agenda?"

So that's where I'd come from. My past with its grand efforts did not look so grand. My total dependence looked partially pathetic.

"Where are you going?" God prodded gently.

Had Moses heard those words as he ran out of Egypt after killing an Egyptian, defending his own race, and getting in a skirmish with two of his kinsmen?

Had Jonah heard those words as he ran for the harbor in Nineveh and conveniently discovered a ship ready for departure? Jonah felt so much peace running away that he slept through a storm at sea.

Had Elijah heard those words when he headed for a cave with the threats of the angry Queen Jezebel ringing in his ears? "I have had enough, Lord," said Elijah as he went to sleep (1 Kings 19:4).

"Ditto," I said.

Scripture gives us 20/20 hindsight on these stories.

Moses returned to Egypt—forty years later and on an unstoppable mission though it took another forty years.

Jonah returned to Nineveh. Uncomfortable transportation accommodations (equally unpleasant for the fish, I assume), but adequate.

Elijah returned to lead his people and to train replacements.

Hagar returned to Sarah to give birth in the household of the one who had mistreated her.

What did these people do with their hurt? How did they muster energy and courage to return to their missions, to pursue their original passions? What is the message for women today, including me?

First, feeling discouraged is not uncommon among people who love God, and in fact, in people who sincerely are doing what they believe they should do. Second, as we read the gospels, we see that Jesus was discouraged from time to time.

It seems to me that discouragement is one of those emotions God uses for teaching purposes. It is not an energizer, like anger. But neither is it poisonous like bitterness. Good can come from discouragement.

Let's see what our 20/20 hindsight will teach us from people who run away.

TRUTH: YOU CAN'T QUIT UNTIL YOUR JOB ASSIGNMENT IS DONE

Moses did leave, finally, leading his sisters and brothers with him.

Nineveh was converted by Jonah's teaching—and God's touch.

Elijah left with pageantry that makes me question that the man riding in an escorted chariot right up to heaven was the same cowardly person hiding out in a cave. However, he had to appoint his successor and complete some generational training first.

I sometimes wonder if our discouragement is connected to our great expectations. The year before I first wrote on discouragement, I had chosen as my verse, "For he performs what is appointed for me, and many such decrees are with Him" (Job 23:14 NASB). I would still caution a woman who chooses her annual verse from Job—unless she has on her spiritual Nikes and is ready to tackle hell.

This year before Christmas, with ten more years of living, I asked God for two simple presents: hope and patience (I was wishing for a year with fewer "things" in it). I have learned more about God's appointments. My annual verse is not from Job. However, I still highly recommend Job's words. They deliver power for us when we are discouraged. I don't want his life, but I treasure his words.

> But if I go to the east, he is not there; if I go to the west, I do not
> find him.
> When he is at work in the north, I do not see him; when he
> turns to the south, I catch no glimpse of him.
> But he knows the way that I take; when he has tested me, I will
> come forth as gold.
> My feet have closely followed his steps; I have kept to his way
> without turning aside.
> I have not departed from the commands of his lips; I have
> treasured the words of his mouth more than my daily bread.
> But he stands alone, and who can oppose him? He does
> whatever he pleases.
> He carries out his decree against me, and many such plans he
> still has in store.
> That is why I am terrified before him; when I think of all this, I
> fear him.
> God has made my heart faint; the Almighty has terrified me.
> Yet I am not silenced by the darkness, by the thick darkness that
> covers my face.
>
> Job 23:8–17

Do you find it incredible that He wants you to come out shining like gold? I believe it because He said it. But I do not see it in my life now.

I wish I could sit with Job today. Here's what I'd say.

"Job, thank you for talking to God with reverent bluntness. Sometimes I'm afraid to be honest with Him—as if He can't read my mind anyway. You said He would do what He would do. And you said you were dismayed. You felt God was against you. I understand, and it scares me.

"I guess the Lion of Judah is not so wimpy that He cannot handle my questions. But really, Job, it's scary to see what is happening in my life. I'm discouraged, troubled, unnerved."

"Tell Him, Miriam," I think Job would say.

Hagar might come and sit beside us.

"Discouraged, sister? Join me after you question Him. We'll talk."

"I failed again, Lord. I thought You wanted me to do this. I've worked hard. I was sure I had my orders straight from You. Hours of work, hours of my husband and I parenting the best way we knew how. And rejection. Look at the days I spent devoting my life to what I thought good moms did. Look at the nights my husband and I have spent praying and waiting up. We prayed; we adopted. We began with four miracle babies. What now, Lord? If we began with a heaven-sent family—which we believed with blind faith at the time—has heaven sagged?

"Lord, Papa, isn't discouragement an emotion that plagues youth with their dreams? What now? I'm almost fifty. Isn't it time for me to get a better read on life? To get a grip; to act like a golden saint, not a spooked sinner who still likes to keep an exit sign in view?"

My discouragement over a rejected manuscript years ago seems minor compared to the discouragement of seeing the death of many of my dreams for my family. As I write about discouragement today, I think women feel it more in the family area of our lives than we did ten years ago. Many of my friends are divorced; many have struggled through getting on their feet financially; many have planned weddings trying to include ex-spouses, step-siblings. The list is endless of the surprises in their lives.

I have no doubt that discouragement is not an emotion for youth only.

I see fresh truth in the verse that I "just happened" on in my daily reading during my run-away season a decade ago.

"These are the nations the Lord left to test all those Israelites who had not experienced any of the wars in Canaan (he did this only to teach warfare to the descendants of the Israelites who had not had previous battle experience): . . . They were left to test the Israelites to see whether they would obey the Lord's commands . . ." (Judges 3:1–2, 4).

God still wants battle-worthy women.

LESSONS OF DISCOURAGEMENT

Do you have a running record like I do? But you haven't given up. Guess what. Refining gold is a process; our one-time victory over discouragement doesn't do it. God left the stuff of the world in His promised land so His people wouldn't become complacent and passive.

I no longer teach weekly Bible studies, so I have not been tested recently, as I was then, by an angry anonymous caller who wished that someone would choke me with those taped teachings. God challenged me to love the person behind the unknown voice.

This present battle is to believe God can bring glory to Himself through my family.

"Miriam, will you love your son in handcuffs?"

"Daughter, do you trust me enough that your youthful blind faith can give way to faith that with mature vision sees a family you did not request? A family that keeps you on your knees. A family that you cannot hold up today as a trophy of unity."

My battle experiences have changed, but God's objective has not. He's still testing my obedience, offering me options, delighted that I'm not a robot programmed to do His will.

What does discouragement teach us?

Lesson 1—Timing

I indulged in some delightful moments of "sisterhood" talk with the Christian mother of one of my students. We shared a memory stroll back to the time our teens were small. She and I both intended to be perfect mothers, excellent employees, frequent church attenders, home care-takers. Her battles have been different from mine. She has never been married and has no extended family for support. I have more children, adopted children, am married, and have caring relatives.

Discouragement has touched us in the same ways.

Our parenting expectations were too high—but we're adjusting. We hope the parenting final exam is postponed indefinitely.

Excellent employee status is an impossibility now. Period. Maybe when our kids are thirty.

Church attenders—well, we try.

God's timing is based on what He created: the twenty-four-hour day, women with two hands and two feet and bodies that require rest. Perhaps it is God's will for you to finish what you've begun, but not immediately. It occurs to me that I will not be a living sacrifice if I kill myself in the process.

Lesson 2—Perspective

Describe what you see when you are discouraged. My friend who is a dynamic Christian called me one morning: "I just want to run away. You should see all my work. I'll never catch up. I've got to get ready to leave town for a seminar." Grateful not to be in her shoes at the moment, I offered lamely, "It'll wait." (Profound spiritual counsel, huh?)

We share a common personality trait: We like to see finished products. We get discouraged when we are behind. When we get blurred tunnel vision, we call each other.

With our 20/20 hindsight, let's look again at the blurred perspectives of one discouraged runner in our Manual.

Elijah thought he was God's Lone Leader in his corrupt nation. He hid from the pressure. God had been using him in earth-shaking, attention-getting, mind-boggling ways—which no doubt was tremendously emotionally draining. While Elijah was hiding, God got his attention with a rock-shattering wind, an earthquake, and fire. But then He whispered in his ear, "What are you doing here, Elijah?"

He sent him back to a quiet job, to train his other leaders and appoint his successor.

"Faithful is He who calls you, and He also will bring it to pass" (1 Thessalonians 5:24 NASB). It is God's choice, not mine.

Lesson 3—Objective

Outcome-Based Christianity:
Action equals blessing
Giving equals material wealth
Do this—and God will do that

What is wrong with this picture? *God is not a business. He doesn't think like we do.* Outcome-based Christianity has been the popular myth of the eighties and nineties. Consider this evidence in Scripture that defies the popular picture.

Mary obeyed, parented her precious Child, and watched Him die.

Hagar obeyed, returned as God asked, was despised, and was asked to leave.

Paul obeyed, traveled about teaching accompanied by fatigue, hunger, threats, beatings, and shipwreck, and eventually was killed.

Faith-based Christianity describes why ordinary people keep going during discouraging times. His objectives are simply invisible at times.

Lesson 4—Focus

People are more important than programs. Measurable numbers are not directly proportionate to God's real work. Henrietta Meers touched a few people's lives. Of those few people, who she inspired with her hospitality and fired with her infectious desire to change the world, a few touched thousands.

Are you discouraged? Has an intolerable person magnetized your focus, drawn you to a place where you feel smothered, starving, or wilting? Perhaps you are locked into circumstances that allow no room for your needs to be met for emotional survival.

Stop and consider that what you see as failure is God's compliment to you. He is saying, "The gold in you is too precious to remain unpolished." God doesn't shape masses and direct history by neglecting individuals.

Consider that even if you are discouraged and wish to run, you cannot tie God's hands. His timing is right. His perspective is balanced. His objective is clear. And His focus is you.

STEPS TO TAKE

1. Keep reading your Bible. Perspective does not come from people-watching. I read in confidence, in desperation, and sometimes when I'm numb. I have searched for answers for my problems and solutions to my unmet needs. In my search, I stumble into such complete God-love that my question doesn't need an answer anymore, and my unmet need shrivels enough for me to live another day.

2. Keep encouraging reminders around you. My friend Boots wears butterflies—rings, designs, pins. They remind her that God is changing her in positive ways. I have mugs from special people and special places. Shells piled near my sink remind me of hikes following the ocean's edge collecting soul-peace. These things are not like rabbit's feet we depend on for success; they have no power of themselves. They connect our emotions to positives.

3. Encourage other people. Being part of their solution rather than their problem lifts you too. My sister, Nadine, is a story-teller: Her household crow, the pet fox, the bull named the General—somehow laughter always sits at her long, crowded dining table. I have a few animal stories myself—but they are better left untold while people are eating.

4. Change your routine. Discouragement often accompanies rut-living. It's like driving a tractor when the two small front wheels get into a little gully on a farm road. I was driving our John Deere, front wheels following a rut, and didn't notice the gully was getting deeper. Oblivious to my rut driving, eventually I could not muscle the steering wheel enough to turn the wheels out of the rut. The road went straight. The gully turned toward a tree-lined river. The good thing was I did not run into the river. The bad thing was I ran into a tree.

While routine, good habits facilitate efficient, productive living, they sometimes keep us from getting a fresh perspective on frustrating circumstances and people.

Jesus climbed in the wilderness hills and was refreshed. I imagine Him absorbing the rugged strength of the rocks, being invigorated by the winds off Galilee.

I know this is a challenge for busy women. Routine which seems like our salvation can blind us to fresh answers when we are discouraged. I can assure you that when I have followed Jesus out of my rut-living the only thing more precious than His teaching is His company.

Hear my voice when I call, O Lord; be merciful to me and
*   answer me.*
My heart says of you, "Seek his face!" Your face, Lord, I will
*   seek.*
Do not hide your face from me, do not turn your servant away
*   in anger; you have been my helper. Do not reject me or*
*   forsake me, O God my Savior.*
Though my father and mother forsake me, the Lord will receive
*   me.*
Teach me your way, O Lord; lead me in a straight path because
*   of my oppressors.*
Do not turn me over to the desire of my foes, for false witnesses
*   rise up against me, breathing out violence.*
I am still confident of this: I will see the goodness of the Lord in
*   the land of the living.*
Wait for the Lord; be strong and take heart and wait for the
*   Lord.*

Psalm 27:7–14

Chapter Ten

. . . .

DEPRESSION:
THE
MISUNDERSTOOD
EMOTION

Depression in women today is:

> misunderstood
> declining
> over diagnosed
> mistreated therapeutically (frequently)
> over spiritualized

Depression is the most misunderstood emotion women experience. This emotion is never a loner; feelings of anger, grief, fear, or anxiety arrive before, with, or after depression. Our confusion usually comes because we don't identify the other emotions that fuel depression. This emotion is part of God's creation in both male and female. But life experiences result in great differences between men and women and how depression affects our lives.

In both women and men, depression is a normal reaction to loss, crisis, or any traumatic event.

The similarity in female and male depression ends with that simple statement and shared symptoms. Life experiences and expectations send women and men in different directions. The causes, actions taken, other people's reactions, and treatment for depressed women and men are very different.

Whereas depression is a normal response to crisis or change, clinical depression is the negative result of not responding to the crisis or not readjusting our lives or our perspectives to change.

In any six-month period 9.4 million Americans suffer from clinical depression, and (according to one resource[1]) one in four women and one in ten men will become clinically depressed during their lifetime. Although these statistics are depressing, most show that the incidence of depression in women has declined over the last fifteen years.

Why does it seem that women are more likely to be depressed than men? I believe that life experiences are primarily responsible for the difference. Also, women go for help more readily, and therefore make up a greater portion of the statistics. I do not believe that women are biologically more prone to depression than men.

My conclusions about depression may be different from what you've heard. But I see through a woman's eyes, read articles and interpret them through my female experience, and draw conclusions filtering all through my female brain.

It is not my intention to be offensive to men in writing this chapter. I compare the experiences of women and men to show *why* women may feel depressed more frequently than men. It is essential that we look with real eyes at the real emotion in our real world.

A young mother may be especially susceptible to depression. There are valid reasons for this. Pregnancy and a nursing child make demands on the body. In our "skinny" culture, she is probably trying to keep her weight down at the expense of her general health. Her sleep pattern is disrupted by her infant's demands. If she has other small children, it is especially difficult for her to get enough rest. She is probably struggling with her identity at the same time, since the feminist movement has so devalued motherhood. Eating habits that sustained her before marriage and motherhood are not adequate now. Sleep habits that sustained her when there were not constant emotional drains from small children are no longer possible or sufficient. Since demands on her time have increased, she may be more likely to reach for quick sugar pick-me-ups and a cup of black coffee, instead of taking time to eat a piece of fruit.

WHAT IS THIS MISUNDERSTOOD EMOTION?

The word *depression* means different things to different people. Psychologists and medical doctors generally agree on the above definition and define it in terms of observable symptoms. They speak of clinical depression (i.e., when the normal reaction to loss, crisis, or any traumatic event intensifies and the symptoms interfere with normal, productive living) which typically includes:

1. moodiness (or sadness)
2. painful thinking (negative thoughts about self, lack of motivation, indecision)
3. physical symptoms of sleeplessness and loss of appetite
4. anxiety resulting in irritability
5. delusional thinking

Since depression is a great masquerader, a person can be depressed and show none of the common symptoms.

The common definition I use has a potentially positive side: Depression is a *normal* reaction to loss, crisis, or any traumatic event.

Have you ever thought of depression as being good? Some women have been taught that it is sin, frozen anger, a childish attitude, or a selfish feeling. If you believe those misguided teachings, you no doubt feel guilty on top of being depressed. Unfortunately, depression can become a more negative emotion for Christian women, because we believe so many myths about it.

My purpose is to address how women can face changes and traumatic events that have triggered depression so we can begin positive living rather than load women down with condemnation.

I believe that God created us with the capacity to experience depression to get our attention when there is extreme change or trauma in our lives. Depression says, "Stop! May I have your attention, please. Something has changed in your life and you need to make a few adjustments!"

Philip Yancey makes a similar point in *Where Is God When It Hurts?* Physical pain has a good purpose. Pain warns us about injury or disease. My friend Gail, who has no feeling from the waist down, took a cookie sheet from the oven and put it in her lap as she sat in her wheelchair. She wheeled across her kitchen to the frosting with her customary goal orientation, forgetting that she had no feeling in her legs. Her burns were just as serious as if she felt the pain.

People with leprosy may wear shoes that rub away portions of their feet. The irreparable damage may have been prevented if the body had been protected.

Depression warns us that we have a rub or hurt somewhere.

Christian women are not immune; traumatic events happen in our lives. You have probably experienced at least one of the following traumas in your life:

> moving to a new location
> loss of someone important to you; intensity varies with:
>> importance—whether parent, spouse, child, or friend
>> how the loss happened—whether it was sudden or preventable, permanent or temporary—death or divorce
>> whether you or others label "fault"
> loss of a job
> loss of physical attributes: strength, appearance
> birth of a child (postpartum blues is depression)
> childlessness (depression frequently accompanies infertility)
> end of an important relationship (not due to death)
> leave-taking of anyone important to you
> child running away, empty nest

destruction of your home (flood, fire, robbery)
loss of financial security
being injured (attacked, hurt)
loss of reputation, power, prestige
loss of a dream

Recent changes in the life-experiences of women have added traumatic events to our list. Although these may not be new, they occur in greater frequency than fifteen years ago.

rape
physical abuse (physical abuse of women occurs most frequently
    in their own homes)
abortion
being sole care-giver of children
being sole provider for children

Although you and I might not have suffered depression due to these, many of our Christian sisters have. I hope by discussing our feelings we will have greater empathy for each other through times of depression even though the event that triggers depression may be different for each of us.

Maybe you have experienced one or more of these issues. Many Christian women have. You can probably find others in your church who have successfully dealt with similar trials. Ask a leader in women's ministries, or perhaps a trusted pastor, if she or he knows someone you can talk to. If no one in your body of believers is able to mentor you through tough times, ask if they can refer you to a supportive organization, small group, or counseling.

I am discovering as I speak at seminars and talk to women in different settings and circumstances that we do not listen well to other people's pain. In a study I am conducting of Christian women, of those who had been raped and physically abused, more than half had not shared that information with anybody in their church. Sisters, this should not be. How can we bear each other's burdens if we don't even know the ones that are most painful?

Let's begin by being willing to listen. We do not need profound advice and wisdom. A hug will do. As empathy grows, we can tell our sister that, though we do not understand her trauma, we are sorry for what she endured and suffered. This may sound simple, but it is profound. Many women have never heard another voice express sorrow for their tragedy. Healing can begin with the simple words, "I'm sorry you suffered that pain."

HOW CAN DEPRESSION BE POSITIVE?

A thirty-five-year-old woman wakes up dreading the day. For years she has been energetic, outgoing, and productive. Now her head has a dull ache that aspirin won't touch. She is sure nothing good will happen. She dreads the night with its long, lonely hours, wondering if sleep will come to relieve her painful memories. Weeks are filled with uncontrollable crying. She fears going where she used to go, seeing who she used to see. What if she starts sobbing in a store, in a restaurant, with her friends? It's better to stay home. She isolates.

What advice might this woman hear?

Some of you have been there. What did people tell you?

"You're a Christian; pull yourself up by your bootstraps!"

"What sin have you not confessed?"

"Counseling? You shouldn't need professional help. You have God. Don't you believe He can help you?"

Remember my successful progress toward Toledo, Ohio, when I needed to go to Michigan? The advice above is like a helpful, well-meaning traveler giving me accurate information to get to Indiana.

Advice that ignores the cause of depression—even from Christian friends, given with good intent—may send a depressed sister to anger, guilt, and further depression that lingers too long to be positive.

Emotional pain leads to physical symptoms. If we ignore the signal depression is sending, a sense of worthlessness and helplessness can become a way of life. Some women can't eat. Others become best friends with the refrigerator. Our emotions can't hurt without our body knowing.

I am the woman described earlier who dreaded each day. I would have kept my secret and stayed depressed had I not discovered that Moses and Elijah felt like I did in their times of crisis. Both went on to finish what God called them to do. The reassuring truth is that Christians experience depression, and they are not marked "unusable" because of it.

In my own experience, my mind and emotions were struggling to mend from crippling experiences in my childhood, experiences I had ignored and stuffed out of reach. As though I had an overload of messy papers stuffed in a small file cabinet, I couldn't close the drawer. I had to put the mess in order. Then I could close the drawer, mark it "history," and get on with living.

My friend Mary, who grew up in an accepting, reassuring home, finds it hard to understand that the mess had to be put in order and that occasionally the file drawer wants to slide open again. That has not been her battle.

Though she does not fully understand because she has not been there, she accepts my hurts as real for me. We seem so ready to minimize someone else's struggle when we have not experienced the same thing. We have a real treasure in friendship when our sister accepts us including our past hurts.

WHAT CAN WE DO WITH THIS MISUNDERSTOOD EMOTION?

1. Accept as fact that events in real living may result in depression. Being Christians does not guarantee us "no trauma" lives. Bad things happen to ordinary, good people. Good things (like a positive move) make ordinary people feel bad—temporarily or occasionally. The stuff of life can bring fatigue, malnutrition, hunger, illness, injury, hormonal changes, and a host of other events that trigger depression.

POSITIVE: Feeling guilty is not piled on top of feeling depressed because we know depression is a normal feeling.

2. When depression waves its flag, pay attention.

Women—in our hustle and bustle—ignore the signals, *and then we crash.* If you have experienced one of the dramatic changes above, sit down, make your favorite tea or coffee, and write a list of what changes might help you adjust to your loss. Do you know women who have their babies and expect to be at full energy in a few days? A few women can be. Most of us need to give our bodies time to recover from the hardest work in the shortest time we'll ever do.

Do you know women who reenter the employment world, having taken time off for bearing a child (or two, or three), and still try to maintain their living space and family dinner as before?

POSITIVE: Self-care is appropriate and necessary. Choosing to take care of yourself helps you make good decisions, adjust, and recover from trauma.

3. Make adjustments—big, small, trivial, gargantuous. Adjust or crash. When we're through changing, in this changing world, we're through. Period.

POSITIVE: Change is an open door to spiritual, professional, and personal growth. God is at work. He trusts your expandability!

TOOLS FOR HEALING DEPRESSION

What is necessary for learning to handle and move beyond depression? Here are a few tools.

1. A Positive Self-Image

People-approval is never enough to give a person a positive self-image. Healthy emotional balance cannot coexist with self-centered, "I must look the greatest" behavior. When we take our need for approval to God, He accepts, loves, and supports us. When we take our need for approval to other people, they cannot love us enough, show us enough acceptance, or give us a basis for worth. We then become angry inside and may even hold grudges against those who did not satisfy us. People simply cannot do what God can do; they cannot supply unqualified acceptance as God does when He sees me in Christ.

I have the right and obligation to see myself as God sees me. I can adopt His image of me as my own or destroy myself, using some other basis for self-worth. Because I am His adopted daughter, through Him I am capable, significant, powerful, worthy.

Women have more difficulty believing they can possess this tool than men. In our real, human experience, it's hard for women to feel they are capable, significant, powerful, and worthy when they are more likely to be poor, underemployed, restricted in influence in their communities, and powerless.

The sad facts of the status of women may not be changed in my lifetime. If they are, I believe it will be through the courage of Christian women.

2. A Healthy Body

One of depression's messages is slow down. Sometimes depression doesn't send a message; it issues an order—rest. Traumatic events drain our energy. Depression accompanies low blood sugar, whether it is continual or temporary. Physical exertion, even for an excellent cause, drains us.

When Elijah ran from Jezebel he was drained by an emotional high, a great victory, then a long flight fueled with anxiety. No wonder he collapsed in exhaustion.

God didn't grab him and order him back to his prophet post. He fed him and let him rest.

God values our bodies. They are important enough to Him that each is an original. We only get one. We can replace some parts, but not the whole thing—in this life.

Can you marshal enough energy to begin taking walks outdoors? You'll feel better. Wild aerobics may have to wait, but beginning with some exercise helps. Biking was therapeutic for me during my period of depression. Getting into a nearby forest preserve was soothing. The river eased hurts from my mind and rolled them downstream. Earthy wood smells crowded out pressure. Others saw the Des Plaines River as dying and polluted. But it was the only river I had, and it still looks good to me today because of its healing memories. Mallard ducks, lazy, hypnotic swirls, a soothing path for autumn leaves: I can still visualize these healing memories.

Depression can bring good results—like taking care of our bodies. I still bike in the forest preserve out of desire, not desperation. The exercise is good, the therapy inexpensive, and the results satisfying.

3. Straight Thinking

Depression plays tricks with our minds. While any emotion has potential power to change our minds, depression can be especially deceptive. Why does this happen?

- The physical connection

Trauma and/or change affects our chemical balance. We know from medical research that stress "bathes the brain" with chemicals. While research has not discovered all the connections, we do know that depression causes us to see our world more negatively. No wonder—something changed! We describe this using colors. "My world looks gray today." "I feel blue."

People who are depressed have different levels of the hormone cortisole. Genetic research suggests that what happens in our brain during life's crises is tied to trait markers on our chromosomes. These physical changes affect how we think. If we ignore this fact, we may make poor decisions while we are depressed. Getting professional help may be necessary in helping us back on the "straight-thinking" highway. Anti-depression medication has helped many through tough times.

- The mental habit connection.

As we listen to other people, we talk to ourselves. We may not be aware of our self-talk because our thinking is complex, but most of us send messages to ourselves. Self-talk can be so loud that we distort what others are saying.

For example, someone says, "You look great." You mumble that you hardly had time to dress, it's a borrowed skirt, it looks better on your daughter than on you.

Or, "Congratulations, you've done a nice piece of work." You say you were just lucky, at the right place at the right time, or if you had done this or that it would have been better.

Sound familiar? You have a mental habit that will keep you from *straight thinking*. I consider myself an expert on the examples above. I spent the first two decades of my life learning that I was dumb and ugly. Compliments can't be true.

Do you have a message tracking in your mind that keeps you from straight thinking? Conscious or hidden, this thought pattern is powerful and effective. Everything is reinterpreted through this track.

During times of depression, these thoughts are louder and more frequent than usual. Common thought tracks of a depressed person are: "I'm no good." "People don't treat me right." "People just want to use me." "How could I have been so stupid?" "I can never recover from messes in my life."

These thoughts monopolize depressed women's minds. They do a subtle takeover and change positive potential of depression into a negative habit. We get stuck in depression—which is not good—and make poor decisions because we're not thinking straight.

What can we do about these mental habits?

First we have to snag them, identify them, *know* them. I have to think about what I am thinking. I cannot correct a bad mental habit if I don't know it is there. Although only you can think about what you are thinking, sometimes hearing someone else's experience helps you snag a mental habit that is negative.

Pat felt like a nobody. As long as she was accomplishing something, she could live with the feeling. She graduated from high school, then college, got a good job, married, and had six children. When her last child was three, her life nosedived into depression. Her friends lectured her on the successes in her life. "Look at these fine, healthy children. Your husband provides for you and is a caring man. Look at your degree."

Then Pat felt guilty for feeling depressed.

She asked herself, "Why do I feel like a nobody?" She thought of her childhood. Her mother had died when she was seven. Her father had been indifferent. She had always been able to attract her stepmother's and father's attention by achievement. Achievement became vital to her surface feeling of self-worth. When she had no measurable accomplishment, she felt worthless.

Now she knew the mental habit she needed to change.

"I *feel* like I'm nobody unless I'm accomplishing something measurable. I *am* somebody to God, because He made me and has a plan for my life. He accepts me whether I'm accomplishing something measurable or not."

Pat's feelings about herself, now based on truth instead of old mental habits, began to change. Pat did not become an instant new person; but she began a process. She could not coax her feelings to change until she got her facts straight.

During depression, it is common for our inner thoughts to become irrational. We make a mistake. We exaggerate it. We see fender-benders as evidence we are terrible drivers. Investments depreciate and we label ourselves financial failures.

It is important that we catch what we are thinking and label the thoughts accurately. We do make mistakes; everybody does. We are human, after all.

Write down your thoughts. Philippians 4:8 gives guidelines for editing those thoughts. Are they true, honest, and just? Are they pure, positive? Can virtue and something good come from that thought? If not, throw it out.

If we don't snag and change mental habits, they will mold us. We become what we think. Women who believe they are dumb and ugly will eventually begin to act as if they are dumb and ugly. If we think people treat us unfairly, eventually we will make them treat us that way.

We can choose to allow depression to twist our thinking. Or we can choose to think straight.

4. An Empathetic Friend

"A [woman] of many friends comes to ruin, but there is a friend who sticks closer than a [sister]" (Proverbs 18:24 NASB). Friends can intensify depression or help you up. Job's friends brought him down. Friends do not have to understand in order to help. *But they do need to allow you to feel what you feel.* Times of depression often reveal our superficial friends and our true friends. True friends sympathize without sending us further down.

Please empathize with your friend if she is depressed. Remember that her pain is real and probably justified. One woman went to her prayer group hurting. She had been battling depression for weeks and felt she was ready to go over the edge. She told her friends she was hurting. They wouldn't believe her. How could she hurt behind her beautiful face? They thought she had the perfect family. They refused her plea for help.

She found comfort for her pain in a bottle. She didn't have to keep explaining and convincing to get warmth and numbness. Alcohol was guaranteed, always available relief from her pain.

What can a true friend say? Use the suggestions in the chapter on grief. We can always say that we are sorry. Be careful about offering advice or saying, "I understand." Few women have walked the same mile in the same shoes. If they have, they had different feet. Total understanding between different humans simply is impossible.

When my friend Gail was paralyzed from the waist down by an accident, she received letters saying that if she just had more faith, she could get up and walk again. Another letter stated that if she would dig out the sin in her life and repent, she would be on her feet dancing. This is not empathy!

A man in the Bible was hurt by bad assumptions like Gail was, though his handicap was different. He had been blind since birth. People asked Jesus, "Who sinned, this man or his parents?" (John 9:2). Jesus told them (my paraphrase), "Neither. It happened so that I could teach you judgmental, coldhearted people a lesson." The lesson Jesus taught by His action was that He came to earth to help hurting, sinful people become whole. He came to help them face their handicap, rather than deny it existed or deny their hurt. Only then could healing and forgiveness come.

Depression is a hurt as real as a fist in the stomach. It helps to say, "I'm sorry you are hurting," "Your parents shouldn't have treated you that way," or "You must miss him, especially at night."

Empathy is holding each other and crying over the human things that happen. It is loving a crumbling person and giving her room to crumble. It's staying there to hold the pieces, whether you can help put them together again or not.

Friendship bathed in empathy is rare, isn't it? If you have this treasure, you may not need the next tool.

5. *Professional Christian Help*

Not all women need professional Christian help during times of depression, but some do. I have heard people say that Christians should never need a psychiatrist. But those same people hurry to a doctor to get an antibiotic for infections or a cast to straighten and protect a broken arm. I thank God for Christian counselors, therapists, and psychiatrists.

Although I could debate the issue here, I will instead summarize my position: Our minds and our emotions are complex. Sometimes we are unable to unravel painful tangles alone. Many times our friends and family members cannot be objective enough to help. They may be part of the pain. So sometimes we do need to consult a professional.

Help from a professional who is not a Christian is limited and may be detrimental if he or she does not respect and support Christian truths. The non-Christian professional is seriously handicapped in helping us establish feelings of self-worth since our entire basis for self-esteem originates from God. He made us uniquely in His image and accepts us as we are thanks to the blood of Christ. If we erase God from the picture, we are beings who happened by accident. We have no purpose in life other than the goals we set for ourselves—and even these are ultimately meaningless, probably selfish, and most likely destructive to ourselves and others.

Without God as our foundation and Creator and Jesus as our flesh and blood example, our brother by adoption who brings us into God's family, how can any self-esteem be established? Jesus' death proves our worth to Him and His Father. We have historical proof of our worth. I know of no other basis for a woman's healthy self-esteem. Self-loathing is not possible when we accept who we are in Christ—how incredible His love is.

If you have no access to Christian professional help and you must see a professional who does not hold your Christian values, may I offer you a word of warning? Secular therapy is tangled with humanistic philosophy. Any practice that violates biblical principles will hurt you. One Christian psychiatrist told of colleagues (not Christians) who had intercourse with female patients to free them from the "hangup" of belonging to only one man. I have a friend whose teenage daughter was hospitalized and assigned to a bedroom of both young men and women. She was encouraged to form intimate relationships with everyone so she would feel accepted. Six months and $24,000 later, she was released with "no marked improvement."

As I write today, I'm thankful that Christian professionals have areas of hospitals for their clients and a wide range of services. While healthcare, insurance, and costs are changing as quickly as I can type into my computer, the good news is that awareness is heightened that Christians need help too.

What help can you get? Psychiatrists can prescribe medication or drugs. Therapists and psychologists can listen objectively, provide insights, and recommend groups, seminars, and reading materials. Whereas a psychiatrist might also provide these helps, she or he is more likely to refer you to another person for those helps.

Social workers and counselors can provide much of what therapists and psychologists provide. They typically have less training— a master's degree rather than a doctorate—but may provide the help you need.

The use of medication, although hotly debated in some groups, is a topic that cannot be overlooked related to depression. Not being a psychiatrist, I do not pretend to be an expert. However, I can offer some facts and information.

Women who are bipolar (experience extreme mood swings, formerly called manic-depressive) are helped by medication (often lithium). Mood swings may be continuous, periodic in annual cycles, or occasional during a lifetime. Medication, for all but 15 percent of the people suffering bipolarity, can make normal living become not just a possibility, but a reality. Antidepressants can be helpful in at least two ways. When depression has created physical, chemical changes in the brain, medication can "intervene" so that a woman (or man) can begin to think straight sooner than the person might have without medication. Also, when traumatic life circumstances cannot be changed at the time—when the crisis or trauma must be "outlived"—an antidepressant can help the person through the difficult time.

Since antidepressants vary, what helps one woman may have negative side effects or simply may not help someone else. Give your doctor specific feedback. Remember, you only get one body this side of heaven.

Check the credentials of any person with whom you entrust your emotional and mental health. Talk to other people. Helping professionals are people too; they have strengths and weaknesses. Choose carefully before you lay your tangled emotions before a person for help with the unraveling process.

Having lived through a more personal crisis since I first wrote this chapter and having worked with hundreds of families as a counselor, I am compelled to add an important word of caution. While professional counseling can help, beware of misplaced expectations.

A competent psychiatrist, therapist, or counselor cannot:
    change your circumstances
    change your past
    change or "fix" your child, spouse, or significant other
    change you

A competent psychiatrist, therapist, or counselor can:
    help you identify sources of your problems
    help you clarify and see additional choices you can make
    validate straight thinking

6. Thankfulness

Does this sound like a pie-in-the-sky remedy for a real disaster? Does this seem like a cheap bicycle vehicle for a trip that requires a Mercedes-Benz? Let me assure you that the value and effectiveness of thankfulness is beyond Mercedes-Benz quality. It is not cheap, easy, or free. And it is a choice we make alone.

Since depression often follows traumatic events, we may accuse God rather than thank Him in the circumstances. (He does not ask us to thank Him *for* disaster.) We can be sorry the event happened. We can visualize or dream what might have been if the circumstances had been different.

If we choose for depression to be positive, we must apply the Romans 8:28 principle: God is big enough and powerful enough to bring good out of anything. My female hero search found the following evidence:

- Corrie Ten Boom thanked God for her years in a concentration camp.

- Kay Coles James thanks God for growing up in the projects of Philadelphia.

- Gail Meister thanks God she can work and travel—in her wheelchair.

- Pat thanks God for her stepmother and father though they could not nurture her.

These heroines have been my mentors showing me how to live thankfully, not just say it. I thank God for my childhood experiences and have a list of positives that have resulted from those years. Thankfulness is a choice to act based on fact before our feelings change. Eventually our feelings will follow.

The Bible tells humans to be thankful; it gave us that message centuries ago. Secular research is now telling us it is "healthy" to be thankful. Popular psychology now admits that if we think right, we'll feel right. (Sounds like Proverbs to me!)

Do you want to feel thankful? Then think thankful. I begin with simple things: I write them down when my emotions are trying to escape from what my mind is beginning to accomplish. Read the list of what you are thankful for out loud to God. When possible, try to imagine different good things that might result from your painful, growing experiences.

STEPS TO TAKE
1. Write down the basis for a positive self-image. Include what God thinks of you. (Ephesians 1:2–8 may help.)

2. Identify what might have caused your feelings of depression. Have you experienced recent changes in your life? Even positive changes may be a factor.

3. What realistic changes could you make in your daily living to help you through the time of crisis or change?

4. What can you do for your body? Write down changes in activity, exercise, or eating habits that would nurture you. Your body is worth the investment of time and planning.

5. Practice tracking negative mental thoughts. Memorize Philippians 4:8 for help.

6. Using Romans 12:3 as a guide, evaluate yourself honestly. What strengths do you have? what weaknesses? What qualities can you make available for God to use?

7. Be an empathetic friend. Be sympathetic when your friend has tough times, empathetic at all times.

8. What good might come from this growing time? Thank God for unseen, unknown potential. Begin thanking Him before you see results.

NOTE
1. Ronald Kotulak, interview with Dr. Frederick Goodwin, director of the U.S. Alcohol, Drug Abuse and Mental Health Administration. Cited in "New Treatment for Depression Averts Relapses," *Chicago Tribune*, 1 December 1993.

· · · · · · · · · · · · · · ·

Hear my prayer, O Lord; let my cry for help come to you.
Do not hide your face from me when I am in distress. Turn
your ear to me; when I call, answer me quickly.
For my days vanish like smoke; my bones burn like glowing
embers.
My heart is blighted and withered like grass; I forget to eat my
food.

Psalm 102:1–4 (A prayer of an afflicted
[woman]. When [she] is faint and pours
out [her] lament before the Lord.)

*Praise the Lord, O my soul; all my inmost being, praise his holy
name.*

*Praise the Lord, O my soul, and forget not all his benefits—who
forgives all [my] sins and heals all [my] diseases, who redeems
[my] life from the pit and crowns me with love and compassion,
who satisfies [my] desires with good things so that [my] youth
is renewed like the eagle's.*

Psalm 103:1–5
(Praise of a thankful woman)

Chapter Eleven

GOOD GRIEF: CONFRONTING LOSS

Could this woman be my mother? The eyes studying my face looked dull and gray instead of soft hazel. The twinkle of recognition was gone. Except for the high cheek bones and a little russet-colored hair, she could have been another woman. Three years of cancer, chemotherapy, and cobalt treatments had destroyed Mama as I knew her.

Grief was what women felt when someone died. Mama was still here. I could stroke her face, smooth her gown, talk to her. Then why the pain? The machines around her made me angry. I was overwhelmed by a feeling of being lost, of having no place to go for comfort. I had no right to grieve yet. Mama was still here.

Generalizations decay. What women learned about the grief process in the past isn't enough for today. And the reasons we grieve have changed significantly. The old lists of why people grieve don't include the realities of our lives.

Adult children grieve when they realize they can never communicate with their parents on an adult level. We see a friend with her parents talking like people fond of each other. We grieve that we never had that kind of relationship. By the time our parents die, we may have nothing left to grieve. The tears are dried, the relationship ended long ago. Others say, "She's keeping it in," when in fact, there's no feeling left.

Divorced women go through a period of grief. Expectations have died. Hope for the "happily ever after" is lost in bills, lawyers —with more bills, questioning children, financial pressure, and lonely night hours—sometimes. Loneliness may have arrived unrecognized and unexpected much earlier than the divorce papers.

One friend, a mother of six children, told me she was a "recovering divorcée." And she feels she'll never fully recover. Not all women feel that way. But I admired her courage and honesty. It helped me recognize a myth I believed: that you eventually "get over it," finish your grief work, and move on. In reality, patches of grief may forever live in the heart of even a strong, effective woman who is living a dynamic, faith-filled life.

We'll look at reasons women grieve today. But first, let's look at how our grief is different because we are female.

FEMALE CONDITIONING

Women internalize what is happening around them more than men. (Call it "sensitivity" or whatever, it's there.)

Women take responsibility for others' behavior more than men. ("He hit me because I was not submissive enough.")

Women assume individual accountability more than men, even when it is not appropriate. (A man and a women get fired. The woman is likely to say, "Is there something about me they did not like?" The man might say, "That's the breaks; they're downsizing.")

I don't believe these differences are biological or even permanent. They are generalizations today—possibly different from those of our daughters or mothers or grandmothers.

FEMALE EXPERIENCES

Women are increasingly the sole caretakers of our children.

Forty percent of female-headed families live in poverty.

Children in these families are impacted in healthcare, educational opportunities, and many other areas of what moms want for their kids.

Women have traditionally been, and continue to be, more involved in the daily lives of their children.

The majority of women today are employed outside their homes, including women who are moms. Most moms return to work outside their home within their infants' first year.

These examples of conditioning and experiences do not exhaust the list of female/male differences that affect grieving, but they are a beginning. Someday I hope to write a book on women's grief because I believe our distinct experiences call out a host of feelings different from men. But this chapter will do for now.

Combine the lists above with a few significant changes in our world including the following, which have a profound effect on a woman and one of her most cherished trusts, her children:

- Spaces where women work, live, shop, socialize, relax, and travel are more dangerous
- Streets and even city parks are increasingly dangerous for children's play
- Schools may be dangerous, ineffective, and unreachable
- Sexual activity has increased among our teens and pre-adolescents

In short, the world is less "kid-friendly" than it was ten years ago. In addition, home is not as safe a place as it used to be for women and children.

Conclusion: Women experience more loss today than ten years ago.

Unavoidably, women grieve these losses. I am learning lots at the lunch table where I work. We have a "women only" table (my in-house board of advisers). Many of us are just beginning to define and express in words the grief we feel due to changes in our worlds we never expected.

Mothers grieve the loss of childhood for their children, some of whom are never free to play in safety.

Mothers grieve the loss of a two-parent family, especially single moms who come to my office struggling with surviving their teenage sons' adolescence.

"A Mother's Right to Grieve" could fill an entire chapter in a book. And I could write it. We became parents with an agenda that is impossible to fulfill, with expectations that seemed ordinary then, impossible now.

We entered the work force with enthusiasm and a fresh perspective. Some of us entered marriage with less than 20/20 vision. Some stayed single, not expecting to feel isolated.

Jesus tells us we will know the truth, and the truth will free us. I believe He is giving us permission to see what we see, feel what we feel. And we will experience freedom in facing and admitting the truth in our lives.

Some women feel an emotional divorce in their marriage while they share the same address, refrigerator, and children. Talking doesn't communicate. Women (and men as well) grieve when their vows of fidelity are broken. Our Christian culture sorts out what's acceptable, good grounds, unforgivable, redeemable. Somehow, when you're in it, those issues just don't matter. But they isolate you to grieve alone.

Parents grieve when their children die. But what do we call the hurt a parent experiences when her child brings the police to the front door? How do we label the feelings of the parent whose child has run away? You diaper, feed, nurse through high fevers, taxi, teach, and love in the best way you know how. And then during some night your wallet, your car, and your child disappear, taking a piece of your sanity and your dreams.

How do we label the feelings of a parent whose child is immobilized? Mother looks into the face of her twenty-five-year-old son, who is unable to lift his hand to blow his own nose. Grief.

Grief was defined as the slow and gradual adaptation to sudden and absolute separation from a loved one. I expanded the definition ten years ago: Grief is our experience when we must adapt to separation from any person who is important to us or a significant change in a relationship. And now I add to all of the above: Grief is the recognition of the death of a dream.

Mother Search

At this time in my life, I must write about another kind of grief from my own experience. If I felt it ten years ago, it was camouflaged.

Women experience a kind of grief connected to our generational experiences: our mothers and our daughters. It escapes into our sister relationships. Although I cannot explain it well or define it, I can tell you how it feels. Women talk about it. It's in us.

My mother, for reasons I still do not understand, lived away from home from my thirteenth year until I left for college. I remember little about family life during those years. I remember school; I remember assuming the mother role, cleaning and doing laundry. I did not think or question; I just did what I had to do. Before that time she had been a typical (I assume—she's the only mother I had) farmer's wife: hard worker, quiet, getting by. I don't remember her as a person.

I do not remember ever shopping with her. I do not remember any conversations with her about the important things of living.

As I look back, I see times of my life, even while she was living, that I went on a mother search. And I was blessed with many older women friends who are precious to me to this day.

But no human ever filled that mother-shaped hole in my heart.

Perhaps that is why I grieved so during her final illness. I could never experience Mama as a person. She was intelligent and had a college degree and a career before she married Papa. She traveled. We have faded pictures of her in wonderful places with her women friends. I never knew that woman.

Was it her way of surviving in her marriage to take her personality underground? Before my first child was born, I did the unheard of thing of inviting just her—not my dad—out to lunch. "Here," I thought, "I will ask her opinions on politics, her worldview, all the 'woman' things."

She said some things that were obviously Papa's opinions; it was a quiet lunch. And I did not find Mama.

My friend Mary talks of trips with her mother to other coun-tries, emotional support through her teen years and college days. I have seen them together. They talk of political candidates, Mary's job and her school newspaper. Her most wonderful, flattering out-fits are often a gift from her mom! I listen and observe in wonder. I delight—secondhand—in their relationship.

Mary has no daughter and she delights in my "Valerie" stories. Mary listens and offers ideas as I sort through trying to keep up with my daughter's educational leaps and relationship adventures.

Is it possible that some of our grief as women has to do with our dreams for a mother-daughter relationship? Either with our mother or with our daughter? Does what we have, or do not have, affect our friendships with other women? I suspect so. I hope we will talk about it more. Generational blessing described in the Old Testa-ment was a source of inner strength and identity to God's people, women included.

Other women have taught me, sometimes by example but of-ten by words, how to mother my daughter. I have no generational resource to reach back to. I watch Mary; I listen to wise women I've discovered on my mother search, and I am incredibly thankful. I believe they have spared my daughter a mother search.

Grief Beyond Prediction

Grief is not a lone soldier. Like an army officer, it calls out a battalion: anxiety, hostility, guilt, anger, and denial. The next squadron may include loneliness and depression. With all its pain, grief is not an evil emotion. Jesus experienced grief. He grieved over hard hearts, and then He became angry. We are not alone with our emotions. He feels with us.

You may find help by reading books that divide grief into stages. Some list three, some five, some ten.

I have listened to friends who grieved losses I have not experi-enced: Doris, whose daughter died suddenly at age eight; Gail, who became paralyzed from the waist down; Opal, whose husband died; two of my sisters, who are divorced. Looking back on my own losses and listening to theirs, I've noticed that we have not followed the stages. In fact, realizing our feelings were different made us fear discussing them.

I prefer to see grief as a process—one that each woman may experience in her own unique way.

Opal felt numb for two months after her husband died. One friend asked her if she really loved him because she didn't cry. (Comforting words to a widow? Silence would have been better.) Two years later she became depressed mourning for her husband. Tears flowed non-stop in grocery stores, in the mission where she sang and played the piano. When they came, they came without respect to others' presence or understanding.

Why does grief vary so much from person to person? We have such a hard time helping each other. You talk, I talk, and we are still unable to understand. Let's give ourselves room, sisters, to be unique grievers.

How strong is our grief? We don't know until we're in it. How valuable was the person lost? How important was the relationship? What was our expectation? Was the loss totally unexpected? Do we feel guilt?

We grieve when the moving van pulls away with our friends, but that grief does not compare to the grief when we see our mother's casket with mounds of dirt around it. The gentle beauty of flowers does not wipe out the darkness of that black hole in the ground.

Divorce grief wiped two years from my sister's life. She lost her job, moved two times, and took time-out from many friendships. Some of those time-outs became permanent.

We have known that men grieve losing their jobs. Women do too. Mortality rates for men are high during the first year after retirement. Grief is a stressful event. Physical illness, common colds, cancer, and heart attacks are more common. Body reserves are used for the work of grief rather than for fighting disease.

Our work matters too. Our work is an extension of us. Most women report in surveys that they gain satisfaction from their work. Most Christian women report that they consider their work part of their ministry. We grieve career stagnation and job losses.

Parents are not supposed to outlive their children. People should die of natural causes, not of someone else's choosing, and especially not of their own. Murder or suicide bring a kind of grief to women that we seldom talk about. I have talked to mothers in my office whose teens have attempted suicide. It is not unusual for families to keep the attempt a secret. Who helps these women carry their burden of grief? They are denied the healing of talking.

Have you heard that time is a healer of grief? In some instances, that's a myth. Healing depends on what happens during that time. Do we give up emotional dependence on what we no longer have? Success is integrating the loss into our lives and finding new resources, not necessarily filling the void, but finding strength to go on. We reorder our lives.

What helps?

- Knowing that grief is normal—letting yourself feel it
- Tears—on their time table
- Giving yourself grieving time and grieving room
- Turning the corner to comfort

When we are told in Scripture we are not to grieve as do those who have no hope, it means we are to grieve in a different way, *with* hope (1 Thessalonians 4:13). When friends tell a parent, "Don't cry, rejoice: Think of your precious child with Jesus," don't expect that they have helped. Heaven's gain is still that dear hurting parent's loss.

Our Book of instruction shows us examples of both God and Jesus grieving. Since we are created in God's image, we grieve; it's normal.

Tears help. David said, "I dissolve my couch with my tears" (Psalm 6:6 NASB). In another psalm, he said, "My tears have been my food day and night" (Psalm 42:3 NASB). We sometimes feel uncomfortable if they come in public, and unexpectedly—but that's how grief works.

When our daughter left for college, I was unprepared for my feelings of loss. It's minor compared to tragic losses, but still I hurt. She had often accompanied me to Jerry's fruit stand. We'd buy seven or eight bags of fresh fruit and vegetables to get through a week. We always bought kiwi for Valerie. She was the only family member who ate kiwi.

The week after she left, I prepared to make my regular trip to Jerry's. My husband said he'd like to go along. (I think he had a premonition—shopping is not one of his favorite pastimes.) Weaving through the aisles, I came to the kiwi. My feet became dead weights. Kiwi. *I don't need to buy kiwi.* My husband materialized from nearby as the tears began to roll.

He just held me. He cried too. I imagine Jerry's other shoppers found it strange that two ordinary middle-aged people would be so moved by kiwi.

As if once was not enough, it happened again—the tears in public thing. This time I was at Dominick's deli counter. After ordering our usual assortment of cold cuts, I looked straight at the man and said, "One half pound of chicken roll," and I started to cry. There was no Valerie at home to eat chicken roll. Charles, my partner in shopping that night, took over courageously, collected our cold cuts, including the chicken roll that nobody would eat, and ushered me away from the crowd at the counter. "They'd understand if they knew Valerie," he assured me, as if I had not made a fool of myself.

Tears: When they come, they come.

Talking may be part of the healing process. People feel they should say wise or witty words. I remember Joe Bayly's comments on people who came to be with him after his child died. One talked to him and tried to say encouraging things. He wished he'd go away. Another came and sat by him in silence. He was comforted and sorry to see him go. Words can sound glib and flat. Good intentions can't replace good listening. Listeners may want to silence a person grieving because grief makes the listeners uncomfortable. "Try not to think about that now. You've got to live for the future."

The truth of that tidbit is that future living depends on putting the past into some kind of livable perspective. We cannot simply leap over grief into the future.

The honesty of children can help us. When my children were small, a wonderful woman, Mrs. King, cared for them while I taught classes or shopped. Her retired husband often came and played catch with the boys and took them on walks, weaving tales as they meandered through the neighborhood. He died suddenly one night. We did not expect Mrs. King to come that next week. She insisted she wanted to do so.

We explained to our children Mr. King's death as simply as we could. We told them we did not know whether Mrs. King would want to talk about it or not.

The day came and faithful Mrs. King was at the door at 7:00 A.M. She stepped in the door alone and we exchanged the usual greetings. Pajama-clad little Robby cocked his head when there was a slice of silence. "King's in heaven now?" Dear Mrs. King's eyes filled and her shoulders relaxed. "Yes," she said with relief. From that moment on there was an openness that put us all at ease.

Grief makes our thinking fuzzy. It is usually wise not to make big decisions quickly while we're grieving. A faithful friend can gently remind us. One of the positives of grieving is that we often discover which friends can accept us simply for who we are. Bare, alone, poor, single, whatever.

Ordinary advice, "Take care of yourself," is good for grieving people. Edna St. Vincent Millay captures our inclination to forget the necessaries.

> Life must go on
> And the dead be forgotten.
> Life must go on
> Though good men die.
> Anne, eat your breakfast;
> Dan, take your medicine.
> Life must go on,
> I forget just why.[1]

We may not really care about our health or our appearance. But energy to care will return in time.

Some women gain comfort from writing down how their lives have changed and how the future may be different. First lists about the future may be tear-soaked, sad, and incomplete. We are never the same after loss. Whether the loss comes through death, divorce, unemployment, disability, bankruptcy, geographical move, broken children, relationship, rape, or abandonment: We are never the same.

I describe the change as *turning the corner to comfort.*

I fear for women who feel they must push straight ahead after loss. Let loss change you. Growth and the ability to reach out to others more meaningfully will be among those changes. Let your life turn. Let your focus embrace your loss.

New activities, interests, new people can only be taken into your life when you have the emotional energy to invest in them. The time does come when you can explore what your changed life can become.

Be encouraged by this reality: Traditionally women have used their personal loss as the foundation for a helpful cause. Women recover and move from those immobilizing moments of grief. Nationwide thriving networks like Mothers Against Drunk Drivers, shelters for battered women, Hull House for children, and a host of other services were birthed by loss.

The mother of six mentioned earlier grieved her divorce, turned her personal corner, and founded an international organization to help women in other countries form companies to market food products, clothing, and native accessories. She networks helping women in media.

She has modeled for me the process described in Scripture. "The God of all comfort, who comforts us in all our troubles, so that we can comfort those in any trouble with the comfort we ourselves have received from God. For just as the sufferings of Christ flow over into our lives, so also through Christ our comfort overflows" (2 Corinthians 1:3b–5).

Grief is a time to pause, turn a corner of life, and move on in a new direction.

STEPS TO TAKE

1. Accept that grief is a normal emotion when we experience loss.

2. Give yourself permission to grieve in your own way, tears included, on your emotional timetable.

3. Talk about your feelings so that you will have a sounding board for making decisions.

4. When you have emotional energy to invest, discover ways to invest your life in new areas: a new career, hobby, class, or other people you can help.

How you can help a friend who is grieving:

1. Let her express the full range of her emotions: denial, guilt (whether valid or not), depression. Don't support false hopes, but do not insist on facing facts she is unable to face yet.

2. Be a good listener. What you hear may be illogical and unrealistic. But it may be real to your friend. When we grieve, we even attack ourselves.

3. Be a sounding board regarding decisions. Gently help her postpone the big decisions for awhile.

4. Stay around. People may flock during the crisis. Some grief is more intense after the shock wears off. When adjustments stare your friend coldly in the face, call and see what she needs. That's the stuff true friends are made of.

NOTE
1. Edna St. Vincent Millay, *Collected Poems*, Harper and Row, Copyright 1921, 1948.

· · · · · · · · · · · · · ·

I cry aloud to the Lord; I lift up my voice to the Lord for mercy.
I pour out my complaint before him; before him I tell my
trouble.
When my spirit grows faint within me, it is you who know my
way. In the path where I walk [people] have hidden a snare
for me.
Look to my right and see; no one is concerned for me. I have no
refuge; no one cares for my life.
I cry to you, O Lord; I say, "You are my refuge, my portion in
the land of the living."
Listen to my cry, for I am in desperate need; rescue me from
those who pursue me, for they are too strong for me.
Set me free from my prison, that I may praise your name.
                                                    Psalm 142:1–7

Chapter Twelve

. . . .

GUILT:
THE QUESTION
PROMPTER

*G*uilt—tenacious, gnawing—the emotion we'd like to sweep under the rug, put in a computer file and forget the command to retrieve it, push to the back of our messy top closet shelf. What's nasty about guilt is that it surprises us in unlikely living spaces. And yet, true guilt is good and God-given.

Guilt is the emotion that forces us to ask ourselves, "Am I doing the right thing?" Like pain in our toes that makes us change from scrunching shoes to the right size, guilt is an essential emotion we can't live without—we can't live in our Creator's image, that is.

I often fear asking myself that question—"Am I doing the right thing?"—because of two possible answers. "Yes," which I like. And then there's "No."

Another answer to the question that I don't like is the third, more ambiguous option: maybe/I don't know/I hope so.

If you are reading this book, you have a definite advantage in discovering whether you are doing the right thing. You are literate; you can read. That means you can read Scripture, which will usually tell you whether you're doing the right thing. Most of the women in our world cannot read.

For centuries women have had to ask men or follow whatever they were taught. Now we can go directly to our Creator, in prayer, reading Scripture.

In the chapter on contentment, we looked at the myth Christians have bought into: outcome-based Christianity. If the outcome-based yardstick creeps into my emotions, I feel guilty when I shouldn't and OK (at least for a while) when I may have done the wrong thing.

Recently I sat with my supervisor for an evaluation. As a counselor in a public high school, I am evaluated in four areas. I would like to be a "superior" person in all areas. Alas, I am not. My lowest rating was in the area that included going to extra-curricular activities at the high school. I don't do that very often. In fact, I'm only "satisfactory" in that area—next to the bottom rating.

I left my supervisor's office focusing on that one area of the four—feeling guilty. Here I am, a Christian striving for excellence, and I'm ordinary. God, as well as my supervisor, must be disappointed.

I escaped to a corner of the library to stare out the window and pray. My guilt evaporated like water spilled on a hot highway. I have a history of making priority lists before God that together we can revise through stages, years, months, days, and sometimes minutes. Since I have four kids, my greatest desire is to be an excellent parent. If that means being an ordinary employee—so be it.

Others may be called to be excellent employees. Go for it! Maybe someday I shall, but not today.

As I stared out that library window, a flock of Canadian geese waddled into view. Somehow they reminded me that all my hours on the soccer sidelines (my sons' games, that is, not my students') were doing the right thing for this woman at this time. Watching my daughter perform in musicals was the right thing. Taking up running when she started track because she asked me to keep her company was the right thing. (I can't tell you how often I prayed for a red light as we ran the streets so I could stop and huff and puff.) God gave me a mental video replay that crowded out guilt.

You are not alone if you struggle with guilt. Are you pulled to feel guilty if your actions don't produce what you wish? Are you trying to accomplish so much that your excellence badge is tarnished wearing certain hats?

I understand.

LOOKING AT GUILT

The solution to guilt begins with determining whether it is real or false. Do you feel guilty because you have cheated someone—you took more than she intended to give you? Are you bitter or jealous? Did you take someone's sense of worth or take advantage of her openness? Are you nursing a grudge? If so, then your guilt is real, because those things violate Scripture. The solution for real guilt is simpler than the solution for false guilt. It is this:

1. Apologize to the person or people you have wronged, if they are aware of the problem.
2. Ask for forgiveness from the individual and from God.
3. Make restitution when possible. Zacchaeus returned fourfold what he had "stolen" from the taxpayers (see Luke 19:8).
4. Go on from there (Philippians 3:13–14: "forgetting what is behind and straining toward what is ahead, I press on").

You may be looking at step 1 and thinking, "But shouldn't we always get it all out into the open?"

We hear that even from popular Bible teachers today: "Whether or not the other person is aware of your hostility or unfaithfulness or envy or hatred, confess it to him/her. Lay it all out on the table. You'll feel so much closer after it's all over." That is indeed one possibility, but a slim one.

There are other possibilities. The person who is unaware of your ill-feeling, upon learning of it may first be surprised and then hurt. If he (or she) is spiritually mature, forgiveness will follow eventually. However, many Christians are not mature. It may be a long time before they are able to forgive, and they may never be able to forget.

In the meantime, you've put a stumbling block in that person's path. Now the other person is tempted to respond to you with dislike, distrust, or anger—to name a few feelings. If the other person involved is not even aware of your problem, is it not better simply to ask God's forgiveness, and to go on from there?

Early one morning my phone rang. A friend needed help. She felt drawn to another man. As a mutual friend, her husband knew him well. She sensed that the attraction was a two-way street. What should she do?

After hearing a radio program, she concluded that she should sit down with her husband and confess her sin to him.

"And what would he do?" I asked.

"Oh! He'd be furious! He'd fuss and fume and no telling what else. It would be weeks or even months before he could settle down and our relationship return to normal."

In our soap opera generation, this sounds like a great way to deal with the problem. Then to make sure "the air was clear" and everything was "out in the open," she could call the man she was attracted to. She could arrange to meet him alone so that she could confess her sin. Maybe it would set an example for him, right? Highly unlikely! Compromising circumstances can be our undoing. (When Jonah wanted to run away, he just happened to find a ship that just happened to have room for him so that he could run away from God.)

The meeting could become an opportunity for the attraction to grow. Then, if their secret meeting should happen to become public knowledge and his wife find out, they would face all sorts of struggles; there would be the opportunity for all four of them to be closer because of all they'd been through together!

We have enough struggles to fight without maximizing the effects of sin. Would it not glorify God more for this woman to confess her sin to God alone?

Having asked His forgiveness, we must then accept it. Feeling worthy of His forgiveness is irrelevant. First John 1:9 says, "If we confess our sins, he is faithful and just and will forgive us our sins and purify us from all unrighteousness." Fact. We simply accept it. In this case, there was no restitution to be made.

For my friend the fourth step in managing real guilt will be the hardest. "Go on from there." Those are such simple words, but how do we live them? The "how to" will be as varied as the unique individuals involved. My friend will probably find it necessary to do much additional praying after that prayer for forgiveness.

Perhaps these couples can continue their friendship. Perhaps not. If the temptation is too strong, the way of escape (1 Corinthians 10:13) may be no more meetings or communication. It would be better to put the friendship on the expendable list, rather than the marriage.

Where can we go for help with this emotion?

READ SCRIPTURE FIRST

The chapter on disciplines includes suggestions. Read what your Creator has to say to you and other people. Scripture uses the word "sorrow" for our word "guilt." There are two kinds of guilt: real guilt and false guilt. Real guilt is constructive because it makes us feel uncomfortable over things we've done wrong or wrong attitudes we hold. We respond with repentance. God forgives and forgets. "For the sorrow that is according to the will of God produces a repentance without regret, leading to salvation; but the sorrow of the world produces death" (2 Corinthians 7:10 NASB).

False guilt is the emotion we feel when we violate some person's expectation of us, or our own expectations, and that expectation is not God's standard. Reading Scripture we learn what God expects, what is His truth, His desires for us.

Results:

1. You will see our Creator's absolute right.
2. You will see our Creator's priorities in gray areas.
3. Our Creator will give you wisdom to make choices.
4. Our Creator will give you courage to act.
5. Our Creator will give you peace to leave the outcome in His control.

TALK TO OTHERS

Talk to Christian women and others who know you/your circumstances.

Results:

1. You will have more information.
2. You will hear different, sometimes fresh perspectives.
3. You gain sister strength.

PRAY

Ask God to show you wisdom to see your life the way He sees it, according to His Word.

Results:

1. God will give you direction.
2. You will find peace.
3. You will gain power.

Women today carry immobilizing burdens of guilt. Recently I was the guest on a radio call-in program related to women's emotions. Burdens of guilt women carried included being unfaithful to their husbands and having had abortions. As the guest on another call-in program related to teens in crisis, all callers were women. They felt guilty because of their young daughters' loss of virginity, crimes their kids had committed, and mistakes they made in parenting.

We carry guilt that is real. We have done things that violate God's absolutes. Sometimes confession is cloaked with the anonymity of a phone line. Sometimes it is in the privacy of a remote corner at a retreat or conference. Sometimes we can only confess to strangers. We are, after all, human.

Dear sister, those things we have done are exactly why Jesus walked to Golgotha, stayed on the cross, and told His Father He'd finished what He came to do. And then He died.

Those things we have done are the reason Jesus did not stay in that hole in the rock where they buried Him; as Paul puts it, if He had stayed dead, "you are still in your sins" (1 Corinthians 15:17).

I say this to myself—may it help you—when I feel guilty for the things I did wrong, I can choose in an instant to feel free from guilt.

STEPS TO TAKE

1. Ask your Creator's forgiveness.

2. Thank Jesus that He died for that specific thing you did.

3. If the wrong you did involved another person, ask that person's forgiveness.

4. If possible, make restitution to the person you've wronged. Zacchaeus, a dishonest tax collector, returned four times the amount he took from people.

5. Ask Jesus to share the power that brought Him to life with you (Philippians 3:10) so you will not live an immobilized life due to guilt.

6. Forget the past and live today, and tomorrow, and forever like a free, forgiven woman (Philippians 3:13–14).

I wish I could promise you that the freedom you feel from guilt after you've taken these steps is permanent. *Freedom* is permanent. Your *feeling* of freedom may not be. The evil one is never lazy. He cannot change the fact of our forgiveness, but he can remind us of things God has forgotten.

Our feeling of freedom from guilt is temporary. The battle is won and God has forgiven and forgotten. But a nagging voice in my mind says, "Miriam, you'll never finish paying for this one." Reading Scripture gives me incredible evidence that when God says, "Finished—Forgiven," He means it.

King Solomon's parents were David and Bathsheba. Wouldn't Abigail have been a better mother for a king? Solomon's temple was built on the ground where David had offered sacrifices to show he was sorry for having a people count—something God had told him not to do. Wasn't there any real estate nearby that was not so blood soaked?

We cannot understand God's choices. He passes over prime candidates for some assignments and uses ordinary people for extraordinary positions. Because we cannot fathom that He forgives, we think He is looking for women marked "marketable," "will stand well under public scrutiny," or "this product has never been opened." Instead, He gathers women who need rewiring or over-hauling and are on some people's "unusable" shelf.

If we think God picks us because we've hidden our weak spots, the truth is He may choose us in spite of them or because of them. Scar tissue is tough stuff. The scar tissue of guilt alone keeps us inflexible, not sensitive to others who hurt, but the scar tissue of guilt treated with forgiveness is tough tenderness. A strong woman emerges who will not give up. Her loyalty to her Forgiver is a fierce bond. She loves much because she has been forgiven much. Her tough tender scars are priceless.

What about that other kind of guilt women feel that is not caused by doing the wrong thing? What about the guilt we feel even after we read Scripture and see that our action is not wrong?

We are probably looking at people's expectations, not God's. For centuries, women have been trained to feel right or wrong by what people tell them. It's no wonder many of us struggle with that today. It's not a new problem.

Jesus had harsh words for the leaders in His time who weighed people down with heavy expectations while they sat with folded hands.

How many little children grow up in a "church" setting, only to reject Christ? What happened? Children often get a good look at those extra burdens instead of at Jesus. Their response is "no." The "extras" only hinder the impact and appeal of the gospel.

How many people are trying to conform to what they think God expects of them? Much false guilt would be pushed aside if we searched the Scriptures to find His instructions. If you are strug-gling with this kind of false guilt, study especially the book of Gala-tians. Paul pointed the Galatians to God's love and grace. It's available for us. Bruce Narramore summarized this in *Freedom from Guilt*: "The law says, 'perform so you will be accepted.' Grace says, 'you're accepted, now you can perform.'"[1]

I sense that Christian women are making real progress in becom-ing free from guilt caused by not meeting other humans' expectations. I think we are making progress based on our inner confidence. God is in us—guiding our choices. For at least a few decades now, women have been studying their Bibles—in groups, classes, and alone. I praise God for study tools and classes from Precept Ministries, Kay Arthur's vision and gift to women. I thank God for Women's Neighborhood Bible Studies, and a host of other Bible-centered ministries. Some that were once large when more women were at home are now small in numbers. But the impact is still growing like a well-tended wheat field. Who can measure the harvest?

Women got into the Word. And it has made all the difference in their world.

STEPS TO TAKE

if your guilt is caused by trying to meet people expectations:

1. Read Scripture first. This gives us courage to stand. You may be called to be a leader in changing what women do.

2. Forgive the people who have placed unnecessary burdens on you.

3. Identify the barbs (people, places, feelings, circumstances) that trigger "people-produced" guilt in you.

4. Set boundaries related to those barbs so you can live in freedom.

NOTE

1. Bruce Narramore, *Freedom from Guilt* (Irvine, Calif.: Harvest House, 1976).

· · · · · · · · · · · · · ·

I remember my affliction and my wandering, the bitterness and
 the gall.
I well remember them, and my soul is downcast within me.
Yet this I call to mind and therefore I have hope:
Because of the Lord's great love we are not consumed, for his
 compassions never fail.
They are new every morning; great is your faithfulness.
I say to myself, "The Lord is my portion; therefore I will wait
 for him."

Lamentations 3:19–24

Chapter Thirteen
. . . .
BREAKING
EMOTIONAL
HABITS

$\mathcal{J}$f emotions are God-given, part of His original package when He created humans, isn't this an unnecessary chapter? A good gift from God should need no fine tuning, need no corrections, need no breaking and retraining. Right?

We wish, don't we.

If you feel that your emotions are always energizing, mobilizing, and a source of power in your real living, this chapter is not for you. I believe that's every woman's goal, and I know some women who are near that goal. They are mentoring other women and have helped people like me by their example as well as their advice and teaching. I thank God for them.

However, in some of our lives, God's good gift of emotions has been tangled. I'll describe how it feels to me. Instead of arms of strength—God-directed power within—helping me reach out to others, my emotions feel like an octopus outside my control and

God's as well. Instead of encouraging, exercising my gifts, and keeping my covenants to God and people, the octopus arms of my tangled emotions smother, confine, and keep me underwater.

How can this be?

Before we can choose effective tools and methods to break bad emotional habits, we need to identify where they came from, what messed God's good idea. We were created right. God says so in Genesis, in the beginning.

Bad emotional habits come from two sources.

OUR CORRECTABLE DEFECT

Your emotional battle and my emotional battle did not begin when we realized our feelings were out of control. They began with our big sister, Eve, and our big brother, Adam. When they rejected God and chose to ignore their Creator, all their offspring followed their pattern, not God's. You and I were born defective. We have "bad genes," a sin nature that infects all of us.

As I was running in the streets yesterday, a car passed me with a bumper sticker that made a significant statement about the car owner (one of the benefits of running, though not always intellectually challenging, is reading bumper stickers): BORN RIGHT THE FIRST TIME.

Hmmm, I thought. My imagination escaped. *If that's the truth, he's a first since Adam and Eve, who actually were never "born." I'd better catch that car and find out how he did it. The entire human race needs the formula.*

In reality, none of us was born right the first time. We do not naturally want to follow God's directions for our emotions or for our actions. That's a problem.

The solution to that problem is to be reborn.

Visualize the Grand Canyon. God is on one side. We are on the other. He loves us, wishes for us, wants to take us in His arms and give us the best He has. But the garbage of the world and of our sin fills the Grand Canyon. There is no way we can swim through it, climb or jump over it, or fly to Him.

Jesus, His Son, comes to our side of the canyon. He steps to the edge.

"Come, Sister." He reaches out to us. We take His hand and step to the edge.

Jesus lays down, flesh to garbage, and becomes a human bridge for us to walk the distance to our Father. God adopts us.

When my husband and I adopted our two sons, a legal transaction authorized that their birth certificates be changed. They have our names, our provisions, and we cannot, by law (nor would we wish to) write them out of our wills. Adoption is a covenant. It's as though John and Rob have been born a second time.

When we walk the bridge of Jesus to God, a new birth transaction happens. Our God-given emotions can be God-controlled. All the potential for good due to our emotions is possible. The source of bad emotional habits, *being born defective*, need not be permanent; because of Christ's death, our sin is a correctable defect.

OUR "STUFF" STACK

The second source of bad emotional habits is the cumulative stack of stuff in our lives and how we respond to it.

Habits can be good. Ninety-eight percent of what we do is habit. The challenge is to keep the good habits and change the bad ones.

In some lives the stack of behavior is pretty good, and the resulting habits are good. No problem.

Consider your good habits. Your alarm goes off at 5:15. By habit your arm reaches through the dark to the near vicinity of the off button. You swing your feet to the floor on the side of the bed with no wall present. Good habit. You methodically brush your teeth.

If you're a commuter, you can get on the right bus or train with your mind on your calendar or while using your portable phone. My drive to work is like automatic pilot, brain-disengaged habit, for which I am thankful. I can listen to tapes, music, teaching, novels. I can listen to the radio. It requires a bit more dexterity to take notes, record ideas, correct make-up, or eat breakfast. But those extras are possibilities because of habit.

Bad habits? I drink too much coffee. A sign by my coffee pot says, "I'm not nervous, just incredibly alert." Whereas a good habit before action is Ready, Aim, Fire, I habitually Fire, Aim, and get Ready to recover from the consequences.

Many of these emotional habits are formed in childhood and become firmly established during adulthood.

Carolyn was a bitter woman. Bitterness became a habit. She expected that people were out to get her. She believed her relatives did not treat her fairly. She expected that car repairmen would do less than needed or more with a high price tag. She distrusted any financial advisers. Every relationship and event in her life was tainted by her bad emotional habit of bitterness. Will bitterness disappear when she becomes a Christian? When she learns God loves her, will she automatically believe that God will supply her needs? Will forgiving those who have mistreated her in the past be a once-and-for-all victory over bitterness?

It is possible. Sometimes God works instantly. But with many of us He does not. He takes us through a process.

Carolyn's habit formed over time as a series of crises rolled into her life. Breaking the habit began by learning God's facts about contentment. This God-given emotion had been derailed by crisis in her life. When she prayed for God to change her, He gave her invisible antennae to be alert to her bitterness the moment it twinged. "There goes my skepticism buzzer telling me to feel bitter. I'm wondering how that person is going to take advantage of me. Jesus doesn't treat me that way. I'm going to expect the best of that person." She ejected bitterness by choice.

An emotional void is never permanent. Something will fill it. She chose contentment. A bad emotional habit can be replaced by another bad emotional habit or by a good one. We choose what will replace our bad habits.

My sister, who is a recovering alcoholic, says that those in her AA meetings learn not to be "dry drunks." A person can stop drinking and still have bad habits including obnoxious behavior. She tells me that lost years of learning to set boundaries and respecting other people are not regained when you commit to sobriety. You learn new habits.

Do you ever believe that you could break bad emotional habits if you could eject some people from your living space? I do. Are *people* part of your "stuff stack"? This topic gets especially tricky because the right answer for one woman in one situation is not right for all women.

We'll talk about this later. But let's begin at the beginning.

Emotional Habits

Emotional habits involve people around us: for better or for worse. People adjust to each other to survive in the same space. My children are able to prepare their own food because I have a high "nuke" rate. Our Christmas fresh broccoli entered the microwave a foot high. It exited at two inches. (Should I serve the quart of cheese sauce beside it or use it as a soup?) My ability to overcook food has resulted in their ability to prepare their own food.

We learn to survive together as we are. A change in us requires a change in them. Though they suffer from our bad emotional habits, at least they know what to expect.

When you break a bad emotional habit, or are trying to, don't expect others' support. Consider it a bonus if it happens. Our motivation comes from keeping our goal before us.

People who successfully change habits have learned how to get help. Often the help is from people who don't live in our space but who have shared our experience. In weight control groups people share ideas, are accountable to each other, applaud every lost pound in the group. Alcoholics Anonymous members are accountable; they help each other identify their times and places of weakness.

When you must eject a bad emotional habit, are there ever people who must be ejected too? Yes, sometimes. People prints on our lives can be intensely powerful: for evil as well as good.

The Bible sometimes uses what we might consider an old-fashioned word. "Flee." Flee evil. Sometimes it's a person as well as a place or a thing. It was right for Joseph to flee from Potiphar's wife.

As we pray and change, some relationships will change. Some people won't want our companionship any more. They may exit.

We need to be careful in making the call of what is appropriate for other women or judging the call they make.

I was tenderized on my judging attitude when I came to a stage in my life when I could not be in my father's company. In order to be strong enough to parent my four children, I had to protect myself from the pain I experienced in his presence and the emotional plunge I took after the contact. The stage lasted two years.

A Christian sister took me to task on the responsibilities of a loving daughter to her parent, no matter what.

While I agreed whole-heartedly with her theory, I could not live it at the time. Had I been more mature spiritually, able to set boundaries, less damaged, maybe I could have lived the ideal. At that time of my life, I could not tell her *why*. I knew, my counselor and my husband knew. My three sisters understood. And God did.

She helped me learn more intimately, with pain, why God tells us to leave the judging to Him. He alone sees and understands the wounded heart.

People prints, given their power, challenge us to choose who we are with. In some Chicago restaurants, where you sit is determined by who you are with. When I go to an antique auction with my sister, I get to sit in front. Auctioneers always want her there because she's such an active card waver. Her overflowing home, garage, barns, farm houses, and antique booths attest to their wisdom in giving her a front seat.

It feels good to be with the right people.

I have heard women say, "She can do better than that." Interpretation: "She's no low life; she should find a friend with better character."

Picture yourself with Jesus beside you in any relationship you have. Is it a comfortable threesome? Is it a good fit with Jesus? Your honest answer will give you insight into the impact of that relationship on your emotions.

Personal Process: God's Usual Method

One of the most common emotional bad habits for a woman is to devalue herself. Often the source of this is an indifferent father. The woman who has had this experience usually believes her husband is indifferent. She will even try to force him into her father's mold, though he loves her and tries to demonstrate that love. Why? Because for eighteen, or twenty, or twenty-two years she learned to live with this kind of masculine image. She has learned how to live with this kind of authority.

To have a man treat her as a person of worth does not fit in with her habit of devaluing herself. She expects her husband to have ulterior motives for giving her attention. She seeks continual proof that she is first in his life. She is threatened by his job, especially if it is a good one. If his job is demanding, she is jealous. She makes impossible demands of him, in order to "prove" that he doesn't really love her.

Do you struggle with feelings of inferiority? Self-love is a paradox. God created us, pronounced His creation good, and then we have this defect—wishing to live without Him, which makes us defective—until we get connected again. No wonder, the evil one plays us the way a cat plays with mice.

For the first seventeen years of my life, I looked in the mirror at a dumb, ugly reflection. What was real? I don't know. Being my class valedictorian didn't change my opinion of myself.

God is not pleased when His daughters believe inferior things about themselves, His creation. Inferiority breeds bitterness (Whom can I blame?), anxiety (What or whom will I mess up next?), and a host of other bad emotional habits, including fear of setting personal boundaries.

Each of us can discover what helps her break the bad habit of feeling inferior. I discovered that I was helped by spending time alone. I cannot explain the connection. I discovered this when my children were small and quite draining; maybe my emotional storehouse was filled by solitude. Perhaps it was because my happiest moments of childhood were spent roaming the hills of southern Indiana alone. Maybe it's because I focus best on God when I'm alone.

Titus 2:4 tells me that I am to love (*phileo*) my children. That's family love, friendly love, not smother love. Sometimes when we study Scripture more closely, dictionary in hand, we learn a new insight that helps us untangle an emotion.

I use this example of my bad habit of feeling inferior for a reason. I want you to know that if you have struggled with a bad habit for years and have not won yet, you are not alone. Ever my greatest struggle, with all my desire to change, I have not reached my goal. In fact, during some seasons of parenting, I stopped following what He had taught me earlier.

At one rugged time when my children were teens, I succumbed to CMS (crumbling mind syndrome), forgot my own needs for spiritual and emotional health, and hit the skids. The only two positive things I did for myself during that season were to get in Scripture every day (desperate and bleary eyed) and run three miles every other day. I ran not for health reasons—I'd given up on my body—but I believe running helped preserve my mind.

Although I have not won this battle, I can tell you one strength God is building in my weakness. In my work at the public high school, I am ever searching and trying new methods to help students who are at risk. I work especially hard with girls who may not get their diplomas. I spend more time with kids who don't believe they can make it. God is producing something good from my struggle with my bad habit of feeling inferior.

Don't forget early simple lessons. You may, like me, need them forever.

Don't forget that God is in the habit of forgiving. Let's practice the habit on ourselves.

Some parts of Scripture have become treasures to me. For example: "If God is for us, who is against us? He who did not spare His own Son, but delivered Him up for us all, how will He not also with Him freely give us all things? . . . Who is the one who condemns? . . . We overwhelmingly conquer through Him who loved us" (Romans 8:31–32, 34, 37 NASB).

Women's feelings of inferiority sometimes come from hardship, persecution, famine, or nakedness, or danger. Women may lack safety, food, money. We may face trouble or be caught in tough circumstances. The original word for hardship means being put by an enemy in a tight, narrow place, straight and hemmed in on every side with no possibility of escape, with the intent of destroying. I know some women who are in that place. Imagine, some of our sisters felt the same way two thousand years ago in Rome.

Through every tragedy God has one objective. He intends to bring us to a stark confrontation of His love and to help us grow to be more like Him. Nothing can come between us.

My friend, while she was in a German concentration camp, was forced to walk naked with other female prisoners before prison guards. Her eyes cringe as she tells me. She says that in that violated moment, she identified with Jesus, His humiliation on the cross. Corrie Ten Boom had the same experience. I have only read of Corrie, but I have seen the emotional healing in my friend's life. She knows so surely that God loves her. She looks forward to the time when God will replace her scarred body, but she knows He loves her now, scars and all.

"My sister, whenever you have to face trials of many kinds, count yourself supremely happy, in the knowledge that such testing of your faith breeds fortitude, and if you give fortitude full play you will go on to complete a balanced character that will fall short in nothing (James 1:2–4, author's paraphrase).

> *Testing* leads to *perseverance*,
> which leads to *maturity*
> which creates women of *character*

What part do our consciences play in emotional habits? A lot! As James Dobson points out in *Emotions—Can You Trust Them?* our consciences are largely a gift from our parents.¹ Since our parents are fallible, sometimes they train our consciences to direct us in ways that coincide with God's principles, but not always. Our consciences remind us of what brought the approval or disapproval of our parents. What if your conscience has learned principles that are not biblical? It is possible to redirect our consciences. "How much more will the blood of Christ, who through the eternal Spirit offered Himself without blemish to God, cleanse your conscience from dead works to serve the living God?" (Hebrews 9:14 NASB). Our consciences are redirected as the Holy Spirit takes God's Word and applies it to our thoughts and feelings.

When you are motivated to change a bad emotional habit, you will have the opportunity. Opportunity will knock in the form of a test. Face your test as God's compliment to you. He trusts you to enter the process to become a woman of character.

STEPS TO TAKE
1. Identify the bad emotional habit you would like to change.
2. What events or thoughts trigger that feeling or bad habit?

3. What choices can you make regarding those events or thoughts (music, places, people, events)?

4. What does Scripture say: instruction, direction, encouragement?

5. List the authorities in your life. Which is most important to you?

6. Choose to place yourself directly under God's authority. Consider that His strength is available to you in changing bad emotional habits and creating new, good habits.

7. How does your personal sense of worth reflect that authority? Remember you are His royal adopted daughter.

NOTES

1. James Dobson, *Emotions: Can You Trust Them?* (Ventura, Calif.: Regal, 1980).

· · · · · · · · · · · · ·

Remember your word to your servant, for you have given me hope.

My comfort in my suffering is this: Your promise renews my life.

The arrogant mock me without restraint, but I do not turn from your law.

I remember your ancient laws, O Lord, and I find comfort in them.

Indignation grips me because of the wicked, who have forsaken your law.

Your decrees are the theme of my song wherever I lodge.

In the night I remember your name, O Lord, and I will keep your law.

This has been my practice: I obey your precepts.

You are my portion, O Lord; I have promised to obey your words.

Psalm 119:49–57

Chapter Fourteen

. . . .

DISCIPLINES
FOR WOMEN
COMMITTED
TO GROWTH

his life is a test. It is only a test. If it had been an actual life, you would have received further instructions on where to go and what to do."

Do you ever fall for this myth? Do you ever *feel* you have no direction even though you *know* God has given you His instruction Book? The evil one is committed to convincing us there are no answers, no hope, and no resources for our demanding ever-so-daily lives.

If you need convincing that the evil one wants you to believe this myth, listen to this story. I have changed the name of this Christian sister to protect her identity.

Robin works as an admitting nurse at a large hospital in a big city. One coworker is a self-avowed witch. He is open about the fact that he belongs to a coven and practices astrology, tarot card readings, and hypnotism. He wears a pentagon engraved on a ring.

Robin sensed that he was interested in her, and she kept her distance. One day when he was eating lunch alone and reading his astrology book, Robin felt compelled to pray for him. As she finished her prayer and picked up her fork to eat, he slammed down his book and stared at her with a look of horror. He picked up his tray and literally ran across the cafeteria and sat down with some other employees.

Several weeks later Robin was reviewing a chart when a dietitian sitting across from her looked up with a peculiar look on her face. Robin turned her head and saw the witch standing with a Swiss army knife just to the left of her head. She asked him to please put the knife away. He complied and walked away.

Later he said to her, "You know, this is only a practice life; if it were real, we would have received instructions." It's interesting, isn't it, how readily we ignore the Instruction Book we have.

Christian women can no longer live the luxury of coasting along on the coattails of our Judeo-Christian heritage. Lifestyle Christianity, parasitic faith, holy-huddle habits, and codependent spirituality just won't cut it.

We have only one option: discipline.

If you are a Christian, you are a disciple of Jesus. He will show you how to be His disciple by training you.

His training program includes these four simple basics:

WHAT	WHY
1. Reading	to learn
2. Fasting	to focus
3. Praying	to communicate
4. Action	to grow

I have no profound wisdom on how to be a world-class disciple. World-class athletes set records; world-class companies corner the market. I am a heaven-bound woman who wants the high honor of being called "servant." What I communicate is simple and basic. Other books on discipline will help you grow further. What I present is a beginning.

READING

For years I have said that I read the Bible every day, not because I'm a disciplined person, but because I'm a desperate one. This is still true. Read when, where, and as much as you can. I read a little Scripture early every morning. I read more as often as I can. Establish whatever habit works for you. Scripture is also available on tapes. You can "read" with headphones.

One morning, facing a jam-packed day, I was tempted to skip my discipling appointment. Jesus reminded me, "What makes you think you have any business facing a day like this *without* beginning with Me?" How true! I stumble and bumble and fall flat on my face on my good days, the days I've begun with Him. Heaven help me (and everyone around me) if I try to get through without His tender morning training time.

FASTING

Do you want to think about Jesus more? Do you want to pray "continually" about a person or problem? Is there a phrase in Scripture that you decide to think about all day?

And then real, ordinary living smacks you in the face, gobbles your minutes, and monopolizes you body and soul the entire day? Disciples are forgetful. Fasting will focus you. When we don't eat, our stomach regularly reminds us that it's empty. Fasting provides prompting. When we feel hunger, we are reminded why we didn't eat breakfast or lunch. We pray. We focus on Scripture. We focus on the need we're bringing to Jesus.

Fasting is a private discipline. Some fast regularly, some at special seasons or during times of need.

While focus is the greatest benefit of fasting, there are two side blessings. We are thankful for food, and we let our bodies know that our flesh isn't in control of our lives.

PRAYER

Prayer is two-way communication. Many excellent books on prayer explain how to pray and give practical suggestions. An excellent beginning is to say the prayer from Scripture Jesus taught

His disciples (Luke 11:2–4). Using His prayer as a model, write your own prayer in a notebook. When I am distracted I write my prayers or talk to God out loud.

Prayer can be shouts of praise chorused by hundreds of people or questions in quiet followed by silence listening for the God of the universe to respond to a human speck—one person in billions through the years of humanity—one person so special that God listens.

ACTION

You and I have heard, "When in doubt, wait." God answers "Yes," "No," and "Wait." If God isn't showing you what to do, wait until His direction is clear, we are told.

I have a soapbox that I must climb on. Christians have been inactive too long, waiting for God to open doors while we haven't even stepped to the door and turned the knob, to see if God has unlocked it.

I say this to myself. I have been silent too long, tolerant of wrong too long, willing to go with the flow too long. I'm a little duck in a little puddle. I have used the excuse that I can't make much difference. I have not been faithful with the little knowledge I have.

Realizing that in my "little duckness" I am still responsible in the puddle where I swim, I resigned from my union at work because my conscience was in conflict. My union was lobbying for issues that violate my faith in Jesus. I called my school district to task with the help of the Rutherford Institute for violating my first amendment rights as a Christian educator.

I don't know the results of my actions or where all the chips will fall. But I do know that God has shown me two more steps of action I am to take where I swim. Both are things I must say that I've never said before to people I don't know personally. Scared? You bet. But more excited than scared.

Taking action means I'll grow. Growing means I'll be a different disciple tomorrow than I am today, someone different. Are you ready to grow?

Try this growth assessment. In the "tanks" pictured, draw a line that shows how full or empty each tank is in your life today.

ASSESS YOURSELF

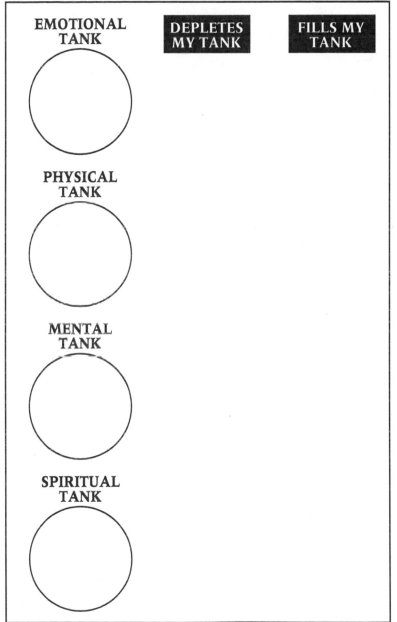

Fill in the blanks under each heading. What depletes your tank?
What fills your tank?

MY PLAN OF ACTION

Lord, I want to grow. Based on what I know of You and Your instructions, my circumstances today, and myself as You have made me, my plan of action is:

To stop/decrease/reduce	To do/increase/add

EMOTIONAL TANK

1.	1.
2.	2.
3.	3.
4.	4.

PHYSICAL TANK

1.	1.
2.	2.
3.	3.
4.	4.

MENTAL TANK

1.	1.
2.	2.
3.	3.
4.	4.

SPIRITUAL TANK

1.	1.
2.	2.
3.	3.
4.	4.

Discipline is a process in growing disciples. Training is never over; we are never finished. We begin by setting our spiritual compass to know God. We discover ourselves, make decisions, and take action. We are never the same. We adjust. We know God in a new way with a fresh relationship. And we go through the process again.

SET YOUR SPIRITUAL COMPASS

KNOW GOD

His Word, His nature

ADJUST ME
priorities,
job, family,
self-care

KNOW MYSELF
skills, abilities, gifts,
personality, values,
needs self-assessment

TAKE ACTION
get training,
knowledge,
develop skills,
"take hold"
prayerfully

MAKE DECISIONS
gather information,
evaluate alternatives,
weigh + and -, make
a plan prayerfully

Why practice these four disciplines?

"Whoever serves me must follow me; and where I am, my servant also will be." (John 12:26)

"If anyone loves me, [she] will obey my teaching. My Father will love [her], and we will come to [her] and make our home with [her]. [She] who does not love me will not obey my teaching." (John 14:23–24)

When Jesus questioned Peter to see if he was ready to be a faithful disciple, He asked him three questions:

"Do you love Me?"

"Do you love Me?"

"Do you love Me?"

This is real life; our world is real lost. Jesus' last words were, "Go and make disciples of all nations, baptizing them in the name of the Father and of the Son and of the Holy Spirit, and teaching them to obey everything I have commanded you. And surely I am with you always, to the very end of the age" (Matthew 28:19–20).

When I was a little girl, Mama would make caramel frosting by cooking all kinds of delicious ingredients in a saucepan. She would set that saucepan in the kitchen window to cool. As soon as it was cool enough to tolerate, I would sneak by and swipe as many fingerfuls as I possibly could before getting caught.

One day, to my surprised delight, I saw the saucepan in the window, with its warm, butter-brown contents. I hadn't known Mama was making caramel that day. In went my fingers for a heavenly mouthful. Arsenic couldn't have tasted worse! Mama's response to my choking and sputtering was that she was making *glue!*

We have lots of emotional freedom as women today. We are encouraged to "tell it like it is." We are encouraged to face our true feelings, to "take our masks off." We are encouraged to give our emotions free rein. Some good may result. But we can eat lots of glue too. Twisted emotions can be uncovered that actually caused less pain when they were submerged. Actions we used to fake were socially acceptable, and what we may really want to do now is not. Doesn't sound like caramel frosting, does it? Our emotions can become a real pit of glue.

Straightening out our tangled emotions need not threaten those around us or throw precious relationships up for grabs. New emotional habits can enable us to become stronger friends, more loving wives, and better mothers. Our renewed, refilled emotional tanks can be sources of vibrant living that are salt to a pretty flat-tasting world.

Our bodies can be better tuned and our intellects can be stimulated. And we can see our emotions as good.

Moody Press, a ministry of the Moody Bible Institute,
is designed for education, evangelization, and edification.
If we may assist you in knowing more about Christ
and the Christian life, please write us without obligation:
Moody Press, c/o MLM, Chicago, Illinois 60610.